DISCARD

The Sy

DATE DUE

D1016638

The Symposium of Plato
The Shelley Translation

Translated by Percy Bysshe Shelley

Edited and introduced by David K. O'Connor

ST. AUGUSTINE'S PRESS
South Bend, Indiana
2002

1 2 3 4 5 6   08 07 06 05 04 03 02

Library of Congress Cataloging in Publication Data
Plato.
    [Symposium. English]
    The symposium of Plato: the Shelley translation
    / translated by Percy Bysshe Shelley; edited and
    introduced by David K. O'Connor.
        p. cm.
    Includes bibliographical references.
    ISBN 1-58731-801-6 (hardcover: alk. paper) –
    ISBN 1-58731-802-4 (pbk.: alk. paper)
    1. Love – Early works to 1800. 2. Socrates.
    I. O'Connor, David Kevin. II. Shelley, Percy
    Bysshe, 1792–1822. Banquet. III. Title.
B385.A5 O25 2002
184 – dc21   2001007275

∞ *The paper used in this publication meets the minimum require-*
ments of the International Organisation for Standardization (ISO)
– Paper for documents – Requirements for permanence – ISO
9706: 1994.

Printed in the Czech Republic by Newton Printing Ltd. www.newtonprinting .com

For Elizabeth, *philtatê philtatôn*:
"It was she who taught me the science of
things relating to Love."

Plato, *Symposium* 201d

For Henry, *philos agathos*:
"Some take pleasure in a good horse or
hound or fighting cock. But as for myself,
I take more pleasure in good friends. With
my friends as partners, I open up and scru-
tinize the treasures the wise men of old
have passed down by writing their books.
If we see some good thing, we point it out
and think it a great gain if we can be useful
to one another."

Xenophon, *Memoirs of Socrates*, 1.6.14

CONTENTS

ACKNOWLEDGMENTS

On the cover is a detail of "Socrates Defending the Fallen Alcibiades," painted in 1828 by Petr Basin (1793–1877). Formerly in the Hermitage, it is now in the Russian State Museum in St. Petersburg. It seems to be one of the few representations of Socrates as a vigorous man in the prime of life, capable of intimidating an enemy or saving a friend, rather than as an old uncle good for little but talk. The event portrayed is reported in Alcibiades' speech (220e). Frederick Crosson brought the painting to my attention, and the image is reproduced with his generous permission.

Bruce Fingerhut, publisher of St. Augustine's Press, has been a patient midwife to this project, and I thank him for it. Debra Nails graciously shared with me her forthcoming work, *The People of Plato* (Hackett), on the historical persons and events of Plato's dialogues (though she should not be taken to endorse the particular claims I make in my note to 172c). My thanks to Robert Williams, for many conversations on all things literary, and also for his help on this project while he was my research assistant. My argument and expression in the introduction profited from the precise editorial eye of James T. Burtchaell, C.S.C., and from the appreciative critical insights of Robert Kunath. All my work on "Plato's Praise of Love translated by Shelley" owes a great debt to my friend and colleague Henry Weinfield, my guide to Romanticism; and most of all to my wife Elizabeth, my guide to romance.

Introduction

> I have seen such beautiful things in the world which, apart
> from desire, I should never have seen. I bless desire,
> the fault of its satisfaction: the fault of the world.
> I bless that fault: that, in its offering
> denying us all, denies us nothing,
> offers the world to us, not to have.
>
> From William Bronk, "Unsatisfied Desire"

The Reader needs no special knowledge to enjoy Percy
Bysshe Shelley's translation of the *Symposium* of Plato (*ca.*

References in the introduction are to the following texts: William
Bronk: *Selected Poems / William Bronk*, edited by Henry
Weinfield, New Directions, 1995. Ralph Waldo Emerson: *Ralph
Waldo Emerson / Essays and Lectures*, edited by Joel Porte, Library
of America, 1983. Milton: *Paradise Lost*, edited by Scott Elledge,
W.W. Norton Company, 1993. Shakespeare: *The Complete Works
of Shakespeare*, updated fourth edition, edited by David
Bevington, Addison-Wesley, 1997. Mary Shelley: *The Complete
Poems of Percy Bysshe Shelley*, edited by Mary Shelley, 1839; reis-
sued in Modern Library Edition, Random House, 1994 [here-
after "1839 *Collected Poems*"]. Percy Bysshe Shelley: Shelley's
translation of Plato's *Symposium* is cited by the bracketed section
numbers and letters (so-called "Stephanus numbers") in this edition; Shelley's unfinished preface to his *Symposium* translation
[hereafter "*Symposium* Preface"] is cited from James A.

427–347 BC), though it does help to be in love. It is a rarity among translations, the work of a master translated by a master.

Shelley (1792–1822) may have first read the *Symposium* as a student, during his brief stay at Oxford in 1810–1811, in the pioneering but erratic English translation of Floyer Sydenham (1767). But he first read the Greek text in the summer of 1817, under the influence of his friend Thomas Peacock, an accomplished classicist and champion of classical literature. The translation was produced the following summer, in July 1818, under curious circumstances.

In March of 1818, Shelley had moved to Italy, in large part to flee the myriad political and sexual scandals in which he had become embroiled in England. Shelley had a talent for such things. Expelled from Oxford at the age of eighteen for publishing a tract defending atheism, he was barely nineteen when in August of 1811 he eloped with his first wife, Harriet. Three years later, with Harriet five months pregnant with their second child, he eloped again, this time with Mary Wollstonecraft Godwin, the daughter of his mentor and supporter, the philosophical radical William Godwin. (Mary was not quite seventeen at the time; she was to write *Frankenstein* two years later.) In November of 1816, Harriet committed suicide, and the following March,

Notopoulos, *The Platonism of Shelley*, Duke University Press, 1949; Shelley's other works are cited from *Shelley's Poetry and Prose*, edited by Donald H. Reiman and Sharon B. Powers, W.W. Norton Company, 1977, verse by line numbers and prose by page numbers. For biographical information, I have also drawn on *Percy Bysshe Shelley: Poems and Prose*, edited by Timothy Webb, J.M. Dent, 1995; and Richard Holmes, *Shelley: The Pursuit*, E.P. Dutton, 1975.

Shelley was denied custody of their two children. He departed from England one year later, and lived in Italy the last four years of his short life. On July 8, 1822, he drowned with a friend when their boat was swamped in a sudden storm. His body was cremated on the beach, and what was believed to be his heart was retrieved from the ashes. His devoted widow Mary kept it in her pillow, inside a copy of the last major poem Shelley completed, *Adonais*, written only a year before as a poetic eulogy upon the early death of John Keats. Alas for romance! Later evidence indicates the organ saved was the liver, not the heart. Yet the sentiment counts for something.

The commotion of the move to Italy had left Shelley unsettled, and his energy for poetic composition suffered a lull. He took up the *Symposium* on July 9, 1818, hoping to immerse himself in the task of translation and revive his spirits. He completed the translation in just ten days. The therapy was successful, and searching Plato's words helped him find himself again. By September he had begun his most original work, *Prometheus Unbound*. Shelley worked on the translation in inspired haste and without the many philological tools now available. He sometimes provided an inaccurate reflection of the Greek, and he made some errors no contemporary scholar would let see print. But it is rare that his errors are seriously misleading, and where they are, the editor's notes should spare the reader confusion.

The *Symposium* translation circulated among Shelley's friends, but he had no hope of publishing it. The homosexual (more precisely, the pederastic) presuppositions of Plato's dialogue, developed most fully in Pausanias' speech (180c–185c), put publication of an accurate translation beyond even Shelley's boldness. But he cared about the translation and kept it in his thoughts. He also was obliged at intervals to retrieve it from his friends. In his last letter – July 4, 1822, almost exactly four years after beginning the translation – he wrote to Mary that he had "found the translation of the *Symposium*," so he may have been thinking about the dialogue again just before he died.

Mary's devotion to the manuscript is all that preserved it. "The English language boasts of no more brilliant composition than Plato's Praise of Love translated by Shelley," she later wrote (1839 *Complete Poems* "Preface" ix). She resisted in every way she could the pressures of Shelley's family and friends to suppress the translation, and tried to get a reasonably representative version into print in her 1840 edition of Shelley's prose works. But censorship had mutilated the corpse, and made the published version more a liver than a heart. Shelley himself had felt compelled to diminish the sexual emphasis of the Greek in a few passages of the translation (see notes to 191c and 210a). But the much more drastic editorial changes in the 1840 edition obscured the erotic theme, for example by substituting "friend" where Shelley had written "lover," and it simply omitted altogether one of the high points of Shelley's accomplishment, Alcibiades' concluding speech, with its story of his failed seduction of Socrates. The translation did not appear in its integrity until the twentieth century.

In addition to his literary talent, Shelley had the right temperament for the task of translating the *Symposium*. Plato himself obliquely characterized the temperament of his ideal reader when he portrayed the eagerness of his own brother, Glaucon, to hear the dialogue's story (see 172c). The *Symposium* tells us no more about Glaucon, but in

Plato's *Republic*, Glaucon is a major character. The conversation in that dialogue reveals Glaucon to possess three psychological traits indispensable for an exemplary initiate into Platonic philosophizing: he is unusually musical, full of erotic passion, and committed to political reform. All three were also prominent features of Shelley's own temperament, and are reflected everywhere in his poetry and his prose. It is true that Shelley's extravagance and lack of discretion made him something other than the prototypical Platonist. But even in this he finds a fair model in the *Symposium* itself, in the charismatic profligacy of Alcibiades, the only speaker intoxicated enough with wine and love to see and tell the truth about Socrates.

The lyrical prose of Plato had no peer in the ancient world, and his investigation of erotic love in the *Symposium* is at once the most searching and the most beautiful in the Western tradition. Plato's story of a drinking-party combines philosophical precision and literary excellence in a style unique and enduring, and every translator must approach the *Symposium* with sandals off. But Shelley has delivered to the English language the light and warmth of Plato's original fire with an authority not since exceeded.

Plato's style is natural without being plain. He avoided the rhetorical artifice that embellished much of the prose of his day, though he could produce fine specimens of this ancient euphuism when it served his purpose, for characterization or parody. In the *Symposium*, the speeches of Pausanias (see 185c with note), Eryximachus (see Aristophanes' comment at 189c), and Agathon (197c) are all markedly artificial, while those of Aristophanes and Alcibiades display a more natural diction, in keeping with their narrative ends and comic sensibilities. Yet as these latter two speeches demonstrate, the register of this natural style can range from earthy colloquialism to ethereal elevation. Socrates' own speech, or rather the speech he attributes to his mentor Diotima, displays the full extent of this range. Teasing or didactic question-and-answer, shorn of any ornament, stands side by side with soaring periods that move into the realm of the prose poem.

But the dialogues do not merely oscillate between low and high. Plato makes the high reveal the potentialities of the low, and lets the low interrogate the pretensions of the high. A word first heard in offhand banter at a dialogue's beginning may reappear and be transfigured in a solemn speech at the dialogue's center; or a sparkling phrase a speaker thinks will show off his profundity may be dragged by Socrates' questionings through the common grit of shoemakers, cooks, and horse trainers, where its false luster is worn away. Perhaps this range is best illustrated for an English reader by Shakespeare's style in the period of his great tragedies. The vulgar gravedigger's quibbles on death and decay, transfigured in the mouth of the sublime Hamlet: in such a creation Plato might have recognized his own stylistic genius.

The Platonic interplay of the earthy and the ethereal, each providing commentary on the other, permeates the *Symposium*. The interplay is set in motion by the dialogue's second speech, by Pausanias:

> Since there are two Venuses, of necessity also must there be two Loves. For assuredly are there two Venuses; one, the eldest, the daughter of Uranus, born without a mother, whom we call the Uranian;

the other younger, the daughter of Jupiter and
Dione, whom we call the Pandemian; – of necessity must there also be two Loves, the Uranian and
Pandemian companions of these Goddesses.
(180d–e)

"Uranian" means "heavenly," while "Pandemian" means
"common" or "popular," which Pausanias wants to reduce
to "vulgar." He intends to make a sharp distinction between
a higher spiritual love that is exclusively male and a lower
love that is bodily and androgynous.

But each successive speaker complicates and unsettles
some aspect of Pausanias' easy dichotomies. First
Eryximachus claims that "the nature of the body contains
within itself this double Love" (186b), undermining the
contrast between orderly souls and disorderly bodies. Next
Aristophanes pokes fun at the supposition that exclusively
male love is superior to androgynous love (see 192a with
note). Agathon joins in by denying Pausanias' claim that
the better love is elder and more sober. Love, asserts
Agathon, "is not only the youngest of the Gods, but invested with everlasting youth" (195c).

Socrates provides the last bit of powder for this gather-
ing explosion of Pausanias' prim segregation of the earthy
from the ethereal. He claims his mentor in erotic wisdom
has been a woman, Diotima: "It was she who taught me the
science of things relating to Love" (201d). Socrates' fellow
party-goers had begun by agreeing to exclude female com-
panionship from their conversation (176e), but the prohibi-
tion is now infringed, first by Socrates in speech, then by
Alcibiades in deed (212c with note to 215c). Diotima further embarrasses Pausanias' dichotomy between the male

and female when she describes the heights of erotic love as a kind of spiritual pregnancy:

> They whose souls are far more pregnant than their bodies, conceive and produce that which is more suitable to the soul. . . . Whosoever, therefore, from his youth feels his soul pregnant with the conception of these excellencies, is divine; and when due time arrives, desires to bring forth; and wandering about, he seeks the beautiful in which he may propagate what he has conceived. (208e–209b)

In this extraordinary image, Diotima retrieves androgyny from Pausanias' manly opprobrium. The divine youth inspired by erotic love seeks in a single longing both the male climax of begetting and the female fulfillment of giving birth.

In a passage that clearly impressed itself on Shelley, Diotima taught Socrates why Love resists being categorized as simply of the earth or of the heavens. Love is fated to be always between the human and the divine:

> [Love] is neither mortal or immortal, but something intermediate – . . . a great Daemon, Socrates; and every thing daemoniacal holds an intermediate place between what is divine and what is mortal. . . . [Love] interprets and makes a communication between divine and human things. . . . He fills up that intermediate space between these two classes of beings, so as to bind together, by his own power, the whole universe of things. (202d–e)

Love is a "daemoniacal intermediate," simultaneously an expression of the human openness to the divine and of our distance from it. We bless desire, in default of its satisfaction.

Shelley was enchanted by the weaving together of the human and the divine in erotic love. Mary Shelley saw this enchantment as one of the defining features of Shelley's personality: "He loved to idealize reality; and this is a taste shared by few. . . . Few of us understand or sympathize with the endeavour to ally the love of abstract beauty . . . with our sympathies for our own kind." Here too is the source of the congeniality of Plato to Shelley, for "in this [love of idealizing], Shelley resembled Plato; both taking more delight in the abstract and the ideal than in the special and the tangible" (1839 *Complete Poems* "Preface" viii–ix). Mary had been a most "special and tangible" wife to her husband, and it must have caused her some pain to recall where Shelley's "greater delight" had lain. But her candid description of Shelley's Platonic sympathies rings true. Shelley found in the *Symposium* a clarifying mirror of his own erotic hopes and anxieties.

Mary wanted to avoid giving the impression, however, that Shelley was a mere student or enthusiast of Plato. She insisted that Shelley's love of idealizing "did not result from imitation." It existed long before "he made Plato his study" in July of 1818 by translating the *Symposium* (1839 *Complete Poems* "Preface" ix). That Mary was right is shown by the immediate effect on Shelley of "making Plato his study." The *Symposium* recalled Shelley to the erotic themes of his earlier work, rather than inspiring him with a wholly new interest.

Shelley actually began to read the *Symposium* in earnest a year before the translation, in the summer of 1817, with his friend Thomas Peacock. He undertook a poem that autumn to celebrate the experience. Its title, "Pandemos and Urania," came from Pausanias' terms for earthly and heavenly love. This poem was influenced as much by Peacock's Platonizing poem *Rhododaphne* as by the *Symposium* itself. Shelley later changed the title of the poem to "Prince Athanase," and finally abandoned it unfinished.

The poem's inferiority justifies Mary's negative assessment of Peacock's influence on Shelley during this period: "[Shelley's] genius was somewhat checked by association with another poet [Peacock] whose nature was utterly dissimilar to his own, yet who, in the poem he wrote at that time [that is, *Rhododaphne*], gave tokens that he shared for a period the more abstract and etherealised inspiration of Shelley" (1839 *Complete Poems* 173–174). But she also saw what was important about this abortive exercise in explicit Platonizing: "The idea Shelley had formed of Prince Athanase was a good deal modelled on *Alastor*" (1839 *Complete Poems* 176 note).

Alastor: Or, The Spirit of Solitude was written two years earlier in 1815, and as Mary said, "none of Shelley's poems is more characteristic" (1839 *Complete Poems* 19). The poem and its preface are an uncanny anticipation of the *Symposium* translation. Indeed, the extensive thematic correspondences and verbal resonances seem to exemplify Ralph Waldo Emerson's description of intellectual influence: in the *Symposium*, Shelley must have felt he had discovered a work of genius in which he recognized his own dearest thoughts, come back to him with a certain alienated majesty (see "Self-Reliance" 259).

The subject of the poem is the spiritual quest of a Poet whose mind "thirsts for intercourse with an intelligence similar to itself." In a vision, the Poet "images to himself the Being whom he loves" (*Alastor* Preface 69):

> He dreamed a veiled maid
> Sate near him, talking in low solemn tones.
> Her voice was like the voice of his own soul.
>
> (*Alastor* 151–153)

This "veiled maid" is an idealization of the Poet's own aspirations, his "unattained but attainable self," to borrow Emerson's phrase ("History" 239). The music of her voice speaks to his own "inmost sense" of "thoughts the most dear to him" (156, 160). These lines describe the culmination of what the preface calls the intense and passionate search of "the pure and tender-hearted" for "human sympathy" (70; Shelley uses "sympathy" where we might say "intimacy" or "mutual understanding").

Shelley's rough magic conjures forth in this vision an atmosphere of apparent narcissism, even of autoeroticism. In the poem's epigraph from St. Augustine (*Confessions* 3.1), the self-involvement of love is enacted in self-involving language: "Nondum amabam, et amare amabam, quaerebam quid amarem, amans amare." ("Not yet did I love, though I loved to love; I sought something to love, loving to love.") Within the poem, this dizzying reflexive turn occurs as the maid's voice and body become instruments of music:

> Wild numbers then
> She raised, with voice stifled in tremulous sobs

Subdued by its own pathos: her fair hands
Were bare alone, sweeping from some strange harp
Strange symphony, and in their branching veins
The eloquent blood told an ineffable tale.
The beating of her heart was heard to fill
The pauses of her music, and her breath
Tumultuously accorded with those fits
Of intermitted song.

(Alastor 163–172)

Shelley's favorite image for the achievement of spiritual intimacy with the natural world was the Aeolian harp, which plays its tune in sympathetic vibration with the natural movements of the wind (see especially "A Defence of Poetry" 480–481). Here Shelley has turned the image back on itself, from one of sympathy with nature into one of a "strange symphony" between the maid's music and her own rising passion. She has herself become nature. The maid's passionate self-interruptions ("voice stifled in tremulous sobs subdued by its own pathos") are also self-expressions, as her beating heart and panting breath are integrated into her song. Phrase and image play together to intensify the atmosphere of Augustinian narcissism, as the maid's music, which is the Poet's vision, becomes a song of the self.

St. Augustine, of course, presented erotic self-involvement as sinful, and suggested that our love of loving could find rest only when reoriented away from self toward its ultimate satisfaction in God. But for Shelley, erotic satisfaction must be sought elsewhere, in what *Alastor*'s preface calls the "prototype" (69).

The prototype is the Poet's idealized beloved. "The vision in which [the Poet] embodies his own imaginations

unites all of wonderful, or wise, or beautiful, which the
poet, the philosopher, or the lover could depicture" (*Alastor*
Preface 69). A fragment written immediately after Shelley
translated the *Symposium* clarifies this idea. "The ideal prototype," he wrote, is "a miniature . . . of our entire self, yet
deprived of all that we condemn or despise," uniting
"everything excellent or lovely we are capable of conceiv-
ing" ("On Love" 473). In other words, the prototype is a
standard by which we measure how far we ourselves have
escaped from "all that we condemn or despise." (The conception of the prototype as a "miniature" within us derives
from *Symposium* 215a–b, where Alcibiades says Socrates is
like a statue of a satyr filled inside with figurines of the
gods.)

It is true, then, that the love of the prototype is a species
of self-love. But it is not mere self-indulgent narcissism,
since it requires an idealization of the self as well as of the
beloved. This sort of self-love is a vehicle for shame at one's
own faults, as well as for disappointment in the faults of
others whom we love. (Here again Shelley is close in spirit
to Emerson's view of friendship and the "unattained self.")
Mary Shelley may have been recalling Shelley's self-criti-
cisms as much as his dissatisfactions with others when she
noted her husband's "endeavour to ally the love of abstract
beauty with our sympathies for our own kind."

The communication between Poet and vision climaxes
in the self-kindled "warm light of their own life" (175).
With her "beamy bending eyes" and "parted lips . . . quiv-
ering eagerly," the maid yields "to the irresistible joy" of
their embrace (179–180, 185, echoed in "On Love" 473).
The Poet rises to the elevation of consummation. But then
the vision dissipates, and he sinks into dispirited languor:

> His wan eyes
> Gaze on the empty scene as vacantly
> As ocean's moon looks on the moon in heaven.
>   (*Alastor* 200–202)

This beautiful passage inverts the myth of Narcissus, who lost himself in rapt contemplation of his own reflection. *Alastor*'s Poet loses himself when he no longer can see himself as a reflection of an ideal beauty. He becomes the empty earthbound shadow ("ocean's moon") of an absent ethereal reality ("the moon in heaven"). The Poet's sympathetic identification with his ideal love, this projection of his own ideal self, is eclipsed in "sudden darkness" when "the vacancy" of his spirit "suddenly makes itself felt" (*Alastor* Preface 69, 70). The Poet loses his grasp on the vision, and "the insatiate hope" awakened by the maid stings his brain "even like despair" (221–222).

So long as the prototype was present to his imagination, the Poet was filled with "visitations of the divinity in man" ("A Defence of Poetry" 505), and could see the possibility of divinity in himself. But our condition is not so handsome as these "best and happiest moments of the happiest and best minds" make it appear. The experience of these moments and visitations proves to be "evanescent" ("A Defence of Poetry" 504), a favorite word of Shelley's. This evanescence and lubricity of all our highest objects lets them slip through our fingers then when we clutch hardest (see Emerson, "Experience" 473).

Evanescence brings a despairing grief as surely as presence brought a divine delight. When the loss of this higher sympathy plunges the vision into "sudden darkness," the lover mourns the compromised reality of his own perfection.

The lover's grief, then, comes only in part from his failure to achieve a sympathetic communion with the imagined beloved. This loss of communion is equally the lover's loss of access to his own higher self. "Love [and] Hope," but also "Self-esteem" are "for some uncertain moments lent" ("Hymn to Intellectual Beauty" 37–38). On this view, the vacancy provoked by the inconstancy of the prototype redoubles the pain of failed sympathy with the shame of humiliated aspiration.

Shelley honored Plato as the discoverer of these "inmost enchanted fountains of the delight which is in the grief of Love" ("A Defence of Poetry" 497). This inter-weaving of delight and grief is the fabric of the *Symposium*, and binds the whole together.

The weave of this fabric appears most directly in Alcibiades' ambivalence toward Socrates. The intoxicated Alcibiades irrupts into the decorous speech-making, bear-ing about him the emblems of Dionysus (see 212e with notes to 175e and 215c). He is torn between a desire to praise Socrates and a desire to censure him (214e, 222a). In the extremity of his ambivalence, he contemplates Socrates' death, and oscillates between considering it as his most fer-vent wish and his most painful fear: "Often and often have I wished that he were no longer to be seen among men. But if that were to happen, I well know that I should suffer far greater pain; so that where I can turn, or what I can do with this man, I know not" (216c). What delight and grief entan-gle Alcibiades in this violent ambivalence?

He begins with delight. Alcibiades praises Socrates for having within himself "images of the Gods," or more pre-cisely little statues or figurines of them (215a–b with note).

The full significance of this conception of Socrates becomes apparent only when Alcibiades returns to it in his peroration:

> If any one should . . . get within the sense of [Socrates'] words, he would then find . . . that they were most divine; and that they presented to the mind innumerable images of every excellence, and that they tended . . . towards all, that he who seeks the possession of what is supremely beautiful and good, need regard as essential to the accomplishment of his ambition. (222a)

In *Alastor*'s terms, these passages treat Socrates as the prototype of Alcibiades' own idealized self. Socrates' virtues are a persistent goad, or perhaps a standing challenge, to Alcibiades' own ambition to seek "the possession of what is supremely beautiful and good."

But Socrates' inward divinity is also obscure, to be glimpsed rarely and with difficulty, and often not at all. The divine images are not visible to everyone or at every time. They show forth only in moments of sudden epiphany (see note to 210e):

> I know not if any one of you have ever seen the divine images which are within, when he has been opened and is serious. I have seen them, and they are so supremely beautiful, so golden, so divine, and wonderful, that every thing which Socrates commands surely ought to be obeyed, even like the voice of a God. (216e–217a).

This evanescence is the source of Alcibiades' ambivalence: his admiration seeks an intimacy that Socrates appears both to offer and to deny.

Since Alcibiades' delight in Socrates is analogous to the delight of *Alastor*'s Poet in the "veiled maid" of his vision, it is not surprising that Alcibiades is also exposed to the evanescence and obscuring "sudden darkness" that provokes the Poet's redoubled grief. He suffers the pain of failed intimacy or sympathy when he tries to convince Socrates to become his lover. He suffers the shame of humiliated aspiration when the divine images of virtue he sees in Socrates no longer seem accessible to him as images of his own idealized self.

The pain of failed intimacy is all the greater because Alcibiades' hopes for it were so high. As he explained to Socrates, "It has been my earliest ambition to become as virtuous and accomplished as possible, nor can I conceive any companion or guide more excellent than you to conduct me in the path of its attainment" (218d). Alcibiades was sure that Socrates could not reject this noble invitation to a love affair premised on an exchange of youthful beauty for mature wisdom.

But reject it he did. Socrates responds to Alcibiades' invitation with his habitual irony. "My dear Alcibiades," he replies, "if what you say of me be true, and if there be any power in me through which you may become better, you must see methinks some very uncommon beauty in me, very different from that loveliness which is so conspicuous in yourself" (218e). Socrates means by this that nothing Alcibiades can offer him, particularly not his sexual favors, will induce him to accept Alcibiades' invitation. But he knows Alcibiades will hear him as agreeing with the premise of Alcibiades' invitation, and so as preparing to accept it. Socrates' irony lets Alcibiades hear what he wants to hear in Socrates' concluding statement, "For the future we will consider what is best to be done; both concerning what you propose, and concerning all other things" (219b). It is not surprising Alcibiades takes this to anticipate their future intimacy, rather than to reject it.

In thrall to his vision of idealized intimacy, Alcibiades casts himself wholly into its pursuit: "I lay the whole night with my arms around this truly divine and wonderful being" (219c). But for Alcibiades as for Shelley's Poet, the humiliating truth only becomes clear in "the cold white light of morning" (*Alastor* 193):

> He despised and contemptuously neglected that beauty which I had thus exposed to his rejection. . . .
> I swear that I awoke and arose from as unimpassioned an embrace as if I had slept with my father or my elder brother. (219c–d)

The consummating embrace with the "truly divine and wonderful being" proves itself a most fleeting visitation of the divine, if not an outright illusion.

When *Alastor*'s Poet awakes from his vision, he pursues "beyond the realms of dream that fleeting shade," his veiled maid, and "wildly he wandered" in the pursuit (*Alastor* 206, 244). This "wandering" (another favorite word of Shelley's) is the fated condition of the erotic idealist. Shelley builds up this theme throughout the *Symposium*. Apollodorus at the dialogue's beginning tells us he had "wandered about," a "miserable wretch," before devoting himself to Socrates (173a); his devotion had not cured him of his wretchedness

(173d), and perhaps like Alcibiades his devotion did not put an end to his wandering. Diotima later says the young man pregnant in soul must be "wandering about" in his urgent search for "the beautiful in which he may propagate what he has conceived" (209b). Finally, Alcibiades "wandered about disconsolately" after his failed embrace with Socrates, in restless pursuit of that evanescent glimpse of those divine images. His sudden vacancy left him "the prey of doubt and trouble," and he became "enslaved to [Socrates] far more than any other was ever enslaved" (219e). Whatever Socratic philosophy did for its devotees, it did not make them settled, and their wandering is another mark of their struggle against evanescence and vacancy.

Simply to be alienated from the intimacy of Socrates was disorienting enough for Alcibiades. But the pain of loss was redoubled by his shame at falling short of his own aspirations to excellence:

> This man has reduced me to feel the sentiment of shame, which I imagine no one would readily believe was in me; he alone inspires me with remorse and awe. For I feel in his presence my incapacity of refuting what he says, or of refusing to do that which he directs. . . . I hide myself from him, and when I see him I am overwhelmed with humiliation, because I have neglected to do what I have confessed to him ought to be done. (216b)

Alcibiades finds his failed intimacy with Socrates to be at the same time an alienation from his own idealized self. Socrates is Alcibiades' prototype of "what is supremely beautiful and good" and of everything to which Alcibiades' "ambitions" drive him (218a, 222d). When he loses Socrates, Alcibiades loses more than what he loves. He also loses his sense of himself as the lover of what he loves. He suffers the redoubled grief of every divorce, for it is one thing to give up a spouse, and quite another to give up being a spouse. This Augustinian labyrinth holds Alcibiades in its wandering mazes. Such is the shame of humiliated aspiration.

Though Alcibiades comes the closest of any single figure in the *Symposium* to the hopes and anxieties of *Alastor*'s Poet, the interplay of Agathon and Socrates is driven by the same issues. Shelley unobtrusively highlights the theme of evanescence in the offhand banter between Agathon and Socrates when Socrates first arrives at the drinking-party.

Agathon invites Socrates to share his couch, in the hope, he says, of getting some wisdom from Socrates merely by touching him. "If wisdom were of such a nature as that when we touched each other, it would overflow of its own accord, from him who possesses much to him who possesses little," replies Socrates, "I should esteem myself most fortunate in reclining near to you. I should thus soon be filled, I think, with the most beautiful and various wisdom. Mine, indeed, is something obscure, and doubtful, and dreamlike. But yours is radiant, and has been crowned with amplest reward" (175d–e). Agathon accepts the ironic praise with good humor, though he warns Socrates of his plan to return to their competing claims to wisdom.

In Plato's Greek, the contrast here is between the public influence and acclaim accorded the wisdom displayed in Agathon's recent theatrical success, and the "insignificant" wisdom of Socrates, which is "as likely to be disputed as the interpretation of a dream." Shelley transforms this into a contrast between Socrates' "obscure" wisdom, which remains "doubtful and dreamlike," and Agathon's "radiant" wisdom.

Scarcely an "inaccuracy," this transformation is a fine insight. Plato's primary contrast is between public persuasion, which may not be truthful, and private truth, which may not be publicly persuasive. The further issue of how evanescent Socrates' knowledge may be is only a secondary theme. Shelley's "obscure" allows for Plato's primary theme: Agathon himself later uses "eminent and illustrious" as the antonym of "unregarded and obscure" (197a). But Shelley foregrounds the secondary theme, and so lets the passage gesture more emphatically toward the later account of Socrates' daemoniacal wisdom, neither pure ignorance nor yet the wisdom of a god (202a, 204a). In particular, he foreshadows Diotima's exhortation to Socrates before initiating him into the "perfect and sublime ends" of Love: "Strain all your attention to trace the obscure depth of the subject" (210a).

Agathon's self-confident claims to erotic expertise are the foil for this Socratic obscurity. He was the youngest and best-looking man at the drinking-party, and his speech begins by characterizing the god of Love in a way that amounts to self-praise:

That [Love] is the most beautiful [of the Gods] is evident; first, O Phaedrus, from this circumstance, that he is the youngest of the Gods; and, secondly, from . . . his repugnance to all that is old; . . . which Love, who delights in the intercourse of the young, hates, and in no manner can be induced to enter into community with. (195a–b)

Agathon is laughing when he says this, but he is not joking. He is presenting himself as the exemplar of Love, and making a claim for his own expertise in erotic affairs, an expertise founded in his poetic art (see 196e) and his ability to create beauty. He is the first speaker to identify himself so boldly with the very god Eros – Phaedrus, Pausanias, Eryximachus, Aristophanes, all were content to present themselves as erotic heroes rather than gods.

Agathon believes of himself and his poetic art what he ends by ascribing to his god:

> Love divests us of all alienation from each other, and fills our vacant hearts with overflowing sympathy. (197d)

This splendid peroration, though not quite a literal translation of Plato (see 197d note), is a pure statement of Shelley's own aspirations for erotic love. He has introduced *Alastor*'s tension between sympathy and vacancy, and resolved it with a youthful optimism appropriate to Agathon. The young and beautiful poet embraces the enchantments and idealisms of love, and refuses his elders' authority and sobriety, those masks of a decrepit cynicism. And as he does so, he looks down on the man sharing his couch, Socrates himself, who is by far the oldest man at the party, and so by the terms of this speech the most alien to love. Agathon makes good his warning to Socrates at the party's beginning that they would find themselves rivals in wisdom (175e and note).

When it is Socrates' turn to speak after Agathon, he takes up Agathon's challenge and produces a counter-myth of his own:

> Love is the child of Poverty and Plenty, [and] his nature and fortune participates in that of his parents.

> . . . Far from being delicate and beautiful, as
> mankind imagine, he . . . is homeless and unsan-
> dalled [compare 174a]; . . . possessing thus far his
> mother's nature, that he is ever the companion of
> Want. But, inasmuch as he participates in that of his
> father, he is for ever scheming to obtain things
> which are good and beautiful. . . . Wisdom is one of
> the most beautiful of all things; Love is that which
> thirsts for the beautiful, so that Love is of necessity
> a philosopher. (203c–d, 204b)

Socrates follows Agathon's lead, and makes the god of Love
into an image of himself. But as befits the aging Socrates,
Love is not, "as mankind (and Agathon) imagine," something delicate and beautiful itself. Socrates' love lacks beauty, but always thirsts for it.

This life of Socratic love is no task for the delicacy and
tenderness of the mere youth of Agathon's competing
vision. The philosopher displaces the poet, and becomes
the exemplar of a "daemoniacal" Love (202e–203a). Tough
and tireless, he pursues beautiful persons and Wisdom herself, but without hope of consummation. Socrates envisions
Love and himself as a phoenix, "neither mortal nor immortal," who "on the same day . . . will at one time flourish, and
then die away, and then . . . again revive" (203e). This is
Socrates' version of the evanescence that haunts Alcibiades
and *Alastor*'s Poet.

The most memorable invocation of the obscurity of
love's desire comes in Aristophanes' speech. Aristophanes
has just said that those in love have "a vain and inexpressible longing to obtain from each other something they
know not what" (192c). (Aristophanes calls the longing

"inexpressible," but not "vain." Shelley has imported into the sentence his own notion of the essential vacancy lurking in love – "vain" and "vacant" come from the same Latin root.) He continues:

> The soul of each manifestly thirsts for, from the other, something which there are no words to describe, and divines that which it seeks, and traces obscurely the footsteps of its obscure desire. (192c–d)

This wonderful sentence is pure Shelley. He liked it so much he used variants of it in key passages of two later major works, "The Sensitive-Plant" and "A Defence of Poetry," as we will see shortly.

The Latin root of Shelley's "footsteps" (we would now say "footprints") is *vestigium*, whence derives "vestige," as Shelley of course knew. "The soul traces obscurely the footsteps of its obscure desire" then means, A lover ("the soul") uses expressions ("traces") that only imperfectly capture ("obscurely") the vestiges in his consciousness ("the footsteps") of his imperfect awareness ("of its obscure") of what he truly desires ("desire," which means "object of desire"). But the paraphrase misses the brilliant way the very structure of the sentence mirrors the structure of its thought. The sentence is nested around "footsteps" at its core, with the coordinated "traces" and "desire" on the periphery, tethered to the core by their qualifying obscurities. Thus is the deep heart's core wrapped about in a triple enigma: the lover's expression of his desire is an imperfect copy of an evanescent vestige of an obscure vision.

Shelley expanded the Greek considerably to achieve this

translation, but he did not distort it. The expansion is based upon a keen insight into the links between this passage and the rest of the dialogue. The phrase "traces obscurely the footsteps of its obscure desire" translates a single word in the original text: Aristophanes says that when the soul speaks of what it really wants, the soul *ainittesthai*. This verb, which is the root of our word "enigma," means to speak "enigmatically" or "indirectly" or "obscurely." It indicates that what the soul says about its deepest erotic desires requires some special mode of interpretation, such as divination, since lovers reach for something that exceeds the grasp of their words. By amplifying this aspect of the text, Shelley makes of Aristophanes an ancestor of *Alastor's* Poet, as he did with Agathon, Socrates, and Alcibiades, offering variations on the same theme of the evanescence of the erotic ideal.

Shelley's image of "footsteps" is derived ultimately from Francis Bacon. Shelley identified the source of the image when he deployed it again in "A Defence of Poetry," in the winter of 1821:

> [The] language [of poets] is vitally metaphorical. . . .
> These similitudes or relations are finely said by
> Lord Bacon to be "the same footsteps of nature
> impressed upon the various subjects of the world."
> ("A Defence of Poetry" 482; Shelley refers to *De
> Augmentis Scientiarum* III.1)

The apparent optimism of this passage, in which poets' metaphors seem to track reality without impediment or veil, is misleading. Throughout "A Defence of Poetry,"

Shelley oscillates between celebration of the power of imaginative language to divine what is real and anxiety over its power to produce pleasing illusions of its own. (Bacon himself displays a similar ambivalence.)

This oscillation between celebration and anxiety is at its most acute near the end of the essay when Shelley returns to the "footsteps" image. "We are aware of evanescent visitations of thought and feeling," he wrote, "elevating and delightful beyond all expression." Their lubricity frustrates our attempts to clutch tight these epiphanies of elevation, yet "even in the desire and the regret they leave, there cannot but be pleasure" (A Defence of Poetry" 504).

This pleasure is as the fading embers' glow to the fire felt by *Alastor*'s Poet in the presence of his vision (see "A Defence of Poetry" 503–504). Yet it is our only lingering access to an evanescent "interpenetration of a diviner nature through our own." The merest vestiges are left us of this Divine Presence:

> Its footsteps are like those of a wind over a sea,
> which the coming calm erases, and whose traces
> remain only as on the wrinkled sand which paves it.
> ("A Defence of Poetry" 504)

The furrows left on the beach by a sea-storm are but a poor record of the glory of the whirlwind. "The wrinkled sand," that is, our consciousness, cannot contain the fulfillment that our erotic ideal had promised. The might of "love, and beauty, and delight . . . exceeds our organs, which endure no light, being themselves obscure" ("The Sensitive-Plant" Conclusion 21–24). Our entry into the milk and honey of our erotic hopes is barred by our conscious mind, and the words that express its calm thoughts. Shelley would agree with William Bronk that desire "offers the world to us, not to have."

This part of "A Defence of Poetry" is in effect Shelley's commentary on "The Sensitive-Plant," a poem he wrote a year earlier, in the spring of 1820. Other than the abortive "Prince Athanase," "The Sensitive-Plant" is in conception Shelley's most directly Platonic poem. It is a much more successful version of that earlier failure, a rewriting of *Alastor* in light of the *Symposium*, now with the translation in hand.

The Sensitive-Plant lives in a garden whose presiding spirit is a kind of Eve or God (2.2–4) to the flowers within it. Itself "companionless" (1.12), the Sensitive-Plant is surrounded by flowers "interpenetrated" by one another's beauty "like young lovers . . . wrapt and filled by their mutual atmosphere" (1.66–69). These young and beautiful flowers are representatives of Agathon's view of love, and their mutual satisfactions are Aristophanic. The Sensitive-Plant, however, is a perfect Socratic:

> For the Sensitive-Plant has no bright flower;
> Radiance and odour are not its dower –
> It loves – even like Love – its deep heart is full –
> It desires what it has not – the beautiful!
>   ("The Sensitive-Plant" 1.74–77)

This is precisely the view of love and of the god Love that Socrates learned from Diotima and taught to Agathon (200a, 204c).

This Socratic lover and its beautiful companions are sustained by the female "Power" (2.1) that animates their mutual relations and ministers to their needs. This Power is analogous to the veiled maid in *Alastor*, and is even described with some similar images, especially when she becomes in herself an Aeolian harp (2.22–24). When she dies, the Sensitive-Plant dies, too, having lost its animating ideal.

In two remarkable stanzas, Shelley describes the relationship between the Sensitive-Plant and the female Power using images drawn from the "footsteps" passage from Aristophanes' speech. The Sensitive-Plant's awareness of this Power comes to it in a kind of vision during sleep,

> In an ocean of dreams without a sound
> Whose waves never mark, though they ever impress
> The light sand which paves it – Consciousness.
> ("The Sensitive-Plant" 1.103–105)

The evanescent dream vision corresponds to the elusiveness of the Power's own presence:

> And wherever her aery footstep trod,
> Her trailing hair from the grassy sod
> Erased its light vestige, with shadowy sweep
> Like a sunny storm o'er the dark green deep.
> ("The Sensitive-Plant" 2.25–28)

Shelley combined these two stanzas a year later to produce the parallel passage in "A Defence of Poetry."

These two stanzas are Shelley's versification of "The soul traces obscurely the footsteps of its obscure desire." In a less compact but still compelling way, they replicate Aristophanes' mirroring in language of the entwined obscurities of the divine object and the human beholder of it. The first stanza shows how obscurely the Sensitive-Plant experiences the Power in the garden. The reality is as "waves" on an "ocean of dreams"; these waves cannot leave "marks" to be read, but only dim "impressions" on consciousness (which Shelley here identifies explicitly with the "sand" of the image). In the second stanza, Shelley makes the divine Power literally cover her tracks, tracks which are already "aery" and "light." She leaves no more accessible or lasting an "impression" on "the grassy sod" than do waves on a sandy beach.

So vestigial are the traces of the divine visitations that the question arises of whether our markings of them are more invention than insight. Shelley's culminating statement in "A Defence of Poetry" hovers around this issue in perfect ambivalence:

> Whether [poetry] spreads its own figured curtain or withdraws life's dark veil from before the scene of things, it equally creates for us a being within our being. ("A Defence of Poetry" 505)

Does the poet probe reality's secret places, or is all the beauty he finds no more than a trick of strong imagination? The disputed question is left undetermined, and with it the fate of the erotic quest. The "being within our being" whose status is left undecided is precisely the prototype sought by Shelley's lovers, a self-idealization. Shelley is here returning to the language we have already seen in the fragment "On Love," language derived from the *Symposium*: the prototype is "a miniature . . . of our entire self, yet deprived of all that we condemn or despise, . . . a soul within our soul" ("On Love" 473–474).

At issue is whether this erotic ideal is an object of Platonic divination or merely of romantic fantasy. What the *Symposium* presents as an incomplete but nonetheless real human openness to the divine, Shelley fears may be an enclosure within the self's imaginative power. Plato would have been pleased by the words William Bronk used to bless erotic desire: "I have seen such beautiful things in the world which, apart from desire, I should never have seen." By contrast, for Shelley there always lurked within love's wandering mazes the awful vacancy of self-involvement. What accounts for this difference between Plato's confidence in the openness of erotic love and Shelley's fear of enclosure?

Shelley's slogan for this self-enclosure was "Nothing exists but as it is perceived" ("On Life" 476; see also "A Defence of Poetry" 505). Shelley was the sort of poet who felt he needed a philosophy, and he played at grounding his fear in an empiricist skepticism derived from Locke and Hume. But Shelley's true emblems of erotic self-enclosure are literary rather than philosophical, and in these two passages he interpreted his slogan by alluding to both Milton's Satan and Shakespeare's Hamlet. This is where he learned the views of creative will and melancholy reflection that served to counterbalance Platonic confidence in erotic divination.

Both of these Romantic heroes exemplify Shelley's ambivalence to imagination's tendency to invention rather than insight. "There is nothing either good or bad, but thinking makes it so" (*Hamlet* 2.2.255–256); "The mind is its own place, and in itself can make a heav'n of hell, a hell of heav'n" (*Paradise Lost* 1.254–55): these brave claims to imaginative self-sufficiency reveal their aspect as curses, too. Hamlet cannot spur his "dull revenge" because his inwardness makes his cause feel to him but "a fantasy and trick of fame" (4.4.33, 61). And Satan's self-glorifying vaunt is echoed back in an abyss of self-despair:

> Which way I fly is hell; myself am hell;
> And in the lowest deep a lower deep
> Still threat'ning to devour me opens wide,
> To which the hell I suffer seems a heav'n.
>   (*Paradise Lost* 4.73–78)

Hamlet and Satan are for Shelley illustrations of the self-consuming isolation suffered by *Alastor*'s Poet at the hands of his own erotic idealism.

When Shelley thought most directly about the erotic prototype and our evanescent vision of it, his skeptical impulse drew him particularly to King Theseus in *A Midsummer Night's Dream*. Consider the italicized phrases in these two passages from the *Alastor* preface and "On Love":

> The vision in which he *embodies his own imaginations* unites all of wonderful, or wise, or beautiful, which the *poet*, the philosopher, or the *lover* could depicture. (*Alastor*, Preface 69)

> If we *imagine*, we would that the *airy children* of our *brain* were born anew within another's. ("On Love" 473)

When Shelley wrote "On Love," revisiting the *Alastor* preface fresh from translating the *Symposium*, he once again had in mind the following italicized phrases from Theseus' famous speech at the beginning of the fifth act:

> THESEUS
> Lovers and madmen have such seething *brains*,
> Such shaping fantasies, that apprehend
> More than cool reason ever comprehends.
> The lunatic, the *lover*, and the *poet*
> Are of imagination all compact.
> . . .
> And as *imagination bodies forth*
> The forms of things unknown, the poet's pen
> Turns them to shapes, and gives to *airy nothing*
> A local habitation and a name.
> Such tricks hath strong imagination
> That, if it would but apprehend some joy,
> It comprehends some bringer of that joy.
> (*A Midsummer Night's Dream*, 5.1.4–8, 14–20)

Theseus here rejects the suggestion of his bride-to-be Hippolyta that the young lovers' reports of their magical erotic adventures may have something of the truth to them:

> HIPPOLYTA
> But all the story of the night told over,
> And all their minds transfigured so together,
> More witnesseth than fancy's images
> And grows to something of great constancy.
> (*A Midsummer Night's Dream*, 5.1.23–26)

Shelley appreciated these romantic sentiments of Hippolyta's, and tried to find something more than fantasy in the enchantments of love. But he also felt the strong pull of Theseus' sober skepticism. Nothing would have pleased Shelley more than to be an Agathon who could "fill his vacant heart with overflowing sympathy" and intimacy. But he got no farther than a half-hearted Socrates, or perhaps an Alcibiades, suspended in the daemoniacal intermediate of a vulgar humanity and an evanescent divinity. Every apprehension of ideal love served to increase Shelley's anguished comprehension of the lower deeps of his vacancy.

"The distinction between poets and prose writers," wrote Shelley, "is a vulgar error, [as is] the distinction between philosophers and poets. Plato was essentially a poet – the truth and splendour of his imagery and the melody of his language is the most intense that it is possible to conceive" ("A Defence of Poetry" 484). This music was at the heart of Shelley's own experience of the *Symposium*. "Plato exhibits the rare union of close and subtle logic, with the Pythian enthusiasm of poetry, melted by the splendour and harmony of his periods into one irresistible stream of musical impressions, which hurry the persuasion onward, as in a breathless career" ("*Symposium* Preface" 402). Shelley aspired to find language of his own that could communicate at least the echoes of Plato's persuasive music, and it is this music that lifts Shelley's version above translations whose prose is tone-deaf to such aspirations.

Shelley's finest accomplishment was to reanimate in English the interplay of the human and the divine in erotic love. He saw that every speaker in the *Symposium* is a mythologist who elevates his own erotic experience into the realm of gods and heroes. Each speech, in rivalry with all the others, presents a different interpretation of what is divine in erotic love.

What conceptions does our time attach to love, what to the divine? One hesitates to pronounce these words in our hearing, lest we profane them with our knowingness. A disenchanted irony chagrins every elevated word we speak today. Can our translations hope to communicate the sacred names of love as Plato understood them?

Shelley commanded a style expansive enough for the task, earthy as a kiss and solemn as a vow. And yet Shelley was keenly aware of how far his accomplishment fell short of his aspiration. He despaired "of having communicated any portion of the surpassing graces of the composition, or having done more than present an imperfect shadow of the language and the sentiment of this astonishing production" ("*Symposium* Preface" 402). "Sounds as well as thoughts have relation both between each other and towards that which they represent. . . . Hence the vanity of translation. . . . This is the burthen of the curse of Babel" ("A Defence of Poetry" 484). We readers are fortunate that Shelley's vanity proved stronger than his despair over Babel's curse. Even if Shelley's *Symposium* be only a shadow of the true Plato – and how could it be more, dear Reader? Learn Greek! – it is at least the true Shelley. And for this, Plato's readers should be grateful.

December 11, 2001
Notre Dame, Indiana

THE BANQUET*

TRANSLATED FROM PLATO

The editor's notes to passages marked with an asterisk (*), keyed to the bracketed section numbers, begin on p. 75.

THE PERSONS OF THE DIALOGUE:*

APOLLODORUS
A FRIEND OF APOLLODORUS
GLAUCO
ARISTODEMUS
SOCRATES
AGATHON
PHAEDRUS
PAUSANIAS
ERYXIMACHUS
ARISTOPHANES
ALCIBIADES

Apollodorus. *[172a]* I think that the subject of your enquiries is still fresh in my memory; for yesterday, as I chanced to be returning home from Phalerum,* one of my acquaintance, seeing me before him, called out to me from a distance, jokingly, "Apollodorus, you Phalerian, will you not wait a minute?" — I waited for him, and as soon as he overtook me, "I have just been looking for you, Apollodorus," he said, "for I wished to hear what those discussions were on Love, which took place at the party, *[b]* when Agathon, Socrates, Alcibiades, and some others met at supper. Some one who heard of them from Phoenix, the son of Philip, told me that you could give a full account, but he could relate nothing distinctly himself. Relate to me, then, I entreat you, all the circumstances. I know you are a faithful reporter of the discussions of your friend; but first tell me, were you present at the party or not?"

"Your informant," I replied, "seems to have given you no very clear idea of what you wish to hear, *[c]* if he thinks that these discussions took place so lately as that I could have been of the party." — "Indeed I thought so," replied he. — "For how," said I, "O Glauco! could I have been present? Do you not know that Agathon has been absent from the city many years? But since I began to converse with Socrates, and to observe each day all his words and actions, three years are scarcely past.* *[173a]* Before this time I wandered about wherever it might chance, thinking that I did something, but being, in truth, a most miserable wretch, not less than you are now, who believe that you ought to do anything rather than practice the love of wisdom." — "Do not cavil," interrupted Glauco, "but tell me, when did this party take place?"

"Whilst we were yet children," I replied, "when Agathon first gained the prize of tragedy, and the day after that on which he and the chorus made sacrifices in celebration of their success." — "A long time ago, it seems. But who told you all the circumstances of the discussion? Did you hear them from Socrates himself?" — *[b]* "No, by Jupiter,* but the same person from whom Phoenix had his information, one Aristodemus, a Cydathenean, — a little man who always went about without sandals. He was present at this feast, being, I believe, more than any of his contemporaries, a lover and admirer of Socrates. I have questioned Socrates concerning some of the circumstances of his narration, who confirms all that I have heard from Aristodemus." — "Why then," said Glauco, "why not relate them, as we walk, to me? The road to the city is every way convenient, both for those who listen and those who speak."

Thus as we walked, I gave him some account of those discussions concerning Love; *[c]* since, as I said before, I remember them with sufficient accuracy. If I am required to relate them also to you, that shall willingly be done; for, whensoever either I myself talk of philosophy, or listen to others talking of it, in addition to the improvement which I conceive there arises from such conversation, I am delighted beyond measure; but whenever I hear your discussions about monied men and great proprietors, I am weighed down with grief, and pity you, *[d]* who, doing nothing, believe that you are doing something. Perhaps you think that I am a miserable wretch; and, indeed, I believe that you think truly. I do not think, but well know, that you are miserable.

Companion. You are always the same, Apollodorus — always saying some ill of yourself and others. Indeed, you seem to me to think every one miserable except Socrates, beginning with yourself. I do not know what could have entitled you to the surname of "The Madman,"* for, I am sure, you are consistent enough, forever inveighing with bitterness against yourself and all others, except Socrates.

Apollodorus. *[e]* My dear friend, it is manifest that I am out of my wits from this alone — that I have such opinion as you describe concerning myself and you.

Companion. It is not worth while, Apollodorus, to dispute now about these things; but do what I entreat you, and relate to us what were these discussions.

Apollodorus. *[174a]* They were such as I will proceed to tell you. But let me attempt to relate them in the order which Aristodemus observed in relating them to me. He said that he met Socrates washed, and, contrary to his usual custom, sandalled, and having enquired whither he went so gaily dressed, Socrates replied, "I am going to sup at Agathon's; yesterday I avoided it, disliking the crowd, which would attend at the prize sacrifices then celebrated; today I promised to be there, and I made myself so gay, because one ought to be beautiful to approach one who is beautiful. *[b]* But you, Aristodemus, what think you of coming uninvited to supper?" — "I will do," he replied, "as you command." — "Follow then, that we may, by changing its application, disarm that proverb, which says, 'To the feasts of the good,* the good come uninvited.' Homer, indeed, seems not only to destroy, but to outrage the proverb; *[c]* for, describing Agamemnon as excellent in battle, and

Menelaus but a fainthearted warrior, he represents Menelaus as coming uninvited to the feast of one braver and better than himself." — Aristodemus hearing this, said, "I also am in some danger, Socrates, not as you say, but according to Homer, of approaching like an unworthy inferior the banquet of one more wise and excellent than myself. Will you not, then, make some excuse for me? [d] for, I shall not confess that I came uninvited, but shall say that I was invited by you." — "As we walk together," said Socrates, "we will consider together what excuse to make — but let us go."

Thus discoursing, they proceeded. But as they walked, Socrates, engaged in some deep contemplation, slackened his pace, and, observing Aristodemus waiting for him, he desired him to go on before. [e] When Aristodemus arrived at Agathon's house he found the door open, and it occurred, somewhat comically, that a slave met him at the vestibule, and conducted him where he found the guests already reclined. As soon as Agathon saw him, "You arrive just in time to sup with us, Aristodemus," he said; "if you have any other purpose in your visit, defer it to a better opportunity. I was looking for you yesterday, to invite you to be of our party; I could not find you anywhere. But how is it that you do not bring Socrates with you?"

But he turning round, and not seeing Socrates behind him, said to Agathon, "I just came hither in his company, being invited by him to sup with you." — "You did well," replied Agathon, "to come; but where is Socrates?" — [175a] "He just now came hither behind me; I myself wonder where he can be." — "Go and look, boy," said Agathon, "and bring Socrates in; meanwhile, you, Aristodemus, recline there near Eryximachus."* And he bade a slave wash his feet that he might recline. Another slave, meanwhile, brought word that Socrates had retired into a neighbouring vestibule, where he stood, and, in spite of his message, refused to come in. — "What absurdity you talk!" cried Agathon; "call him, and do not leave him till he comes." — [b] "Leave him alone, by all means," said Aristodemus; "it is customary with him sometimes to retire in this way and stand wherever it may chance. He will come presently, I do not doubt; do not disturb him." — "Well, be it as you will," said Agathon; "as it is, you boys, bring supper for the rest; put before us what you will, for I resolved that there should be no master of the feast. [c] Consider me and these my friends, as guests, whom you have invited to supper, and serve them so that we may commend you."

After this they began supper, but Socrates did not come in. Agathon ordered him to be called, but Aristodemus perpetually forbade it. At last he came in, much about the middle of supper, not having delayed so long as was his custom.* Agathon (who happened to be reclining at the end of the table, and alone,) said, as he entered, "Come hither, Socrates, and sit down by me; so that by the mere touch of one so wise as you are, [d] I may enjoy the fruit of thy meditations in the vestibule; for, I well know, you would not have departed till you had discovered and secured it."

Socrates, having sate down as he was desired, replied, "It would be well, Agathon, if wisdom were of such a nature as that when we touched each other, it would overflow of its own accord, from him who possesses much to him who possesses little; like the water in the two chalices, which will flow through a flock of wool from the fuller into the emptier, until both are equal. [e] If wisdom had this property, I should esteem myself most fortunate in reclining near to you. I should thus soon be filled, I think, with the most beautiful and various wisdom. Mine, indeed, is something obscure, and doubtful, and dreamlike. But yours is radiant, and has been crowned with amplest reward; for though you are yet so young, it shone forth from you, and became so manifest yesterday, that more than 30,000 Greeks can bear testimony to its excellence and loveliness." — "You are laughing at me, Socrates," said Agathon; "but you and I will decide this controversy about wisdom by and bye, taking Bacchus for our judge.* At present turn to your supper."

[176a] After Socrates and the rest had finished supper, and had reclined back on their couches, and the libations had been poured forth, and they had sung hymns to the God, and all other rites which are customary had been performed, they turned to drinking. Then Pausanias made this kind of proposal. "Come, my friends," said he, "in what manner will it be pleasantest for us to drink? I must confess to you that, in reality, I am not very well from the wine we drank last night and I have some need of intermission. I suspect that most of you are in the same condition, for you were here yesterday. *[b]* Now, consider how we shall drink most easily and comfortably."

"'Tis a good proposal, Pausanias," said Aristophanes, "to contrive, in some way or other, to place moderation in our cups. I was one of those who were drenched last night." — Eryximachus, the son of Acumenus, hearing this, said: "I am of your opinion; I only wish to know one thing — whether Agathon is in the humour for hard drinking?" — "Not at all," replied Agathon; "I confess that I am not able to drink much this evening." — *[c]* "It is an excellent thing for us," replied Eryximachus — "I mean myself, Aristodemus, Phaedrus, and these others — if you, who are such invincible drinkers,* now refuse to drink. I ought to except Socrates, for he is capable of drinking everything or nothing; and whatever we shall determine will equally suit him. Since, then, no one present has any desire to drink much wine, I shall perhaps give less offence if I declare the nature of drunkenness. [d] The science of medicine teaches us that drunkenness is very pernicious; nor would I willingly choose to drink immoderately myself, or counsel another to do so, especially if he had been drunk the night before." — "Yes," said Phaedrus, the Myrinusian, interrupting him, "I have been accustomed to confide in you, especially in your directions concerning medicine; and I would now willingly do so, if the rest will do the same." [e] All then agreed that they would drink at this present banquet not for drunkenness but for pleasure.

"Since, then," said Eryximachus, "it is decided that no one shall be compelled to drink more than he pleases, I think that we may as well send away the flute-player to play to herself; or, if she likes, to the women within. Let us devote the present occasion to conversation between ourselves, and if you wish, I will propose to you what shall be the subject of our discussions." [177a] All present desired and entreated that he would explain. — "The exordium of my speech," said Eryximachus, "will be in the style of the *Melanippe* of Euripides, for 'the story which I am about to tell belongs not to me,' but to Phaedrus. Phaedrus has often indignantly complained to me, saying — 'Is it not strange, Eryximachus, that there are innumerable hymns and paeans composed for the other Gods, [b] but that not one of the many poets who spring up in the world has ever composed a verse in honour of Love, who is such and so great a God? Nor any one of those accomplished sophists, who, like the famous Prodicus, have celebrated the praise of Hercules and others, has ever celebrated that of Love; but what is more astonishing, I have lately met with the book of some philosopher, in which salt is celebrated on account of its utility, and many other things of the same nature are in like manner celebrated with elaborate praise. *[c]* That so much serious thought is expended on such trifles, and that no man has dared to this day to frame a hymn in honour of Love, who being so great a deity, is thus neglected, may well be sufficient to excite my indignation.'

"There seemed to me some justice in these complaints of Phaedrus; I propose, therefore, at the same time, for the sake of giving pleasure to Phaedrus, and that we may on the present occasion do something well and befitting us, that this God should receive from those who are now present the honour which is most due to him. *[d]* If you agree to my proposal, an excellent discussion might arise on the subject. Every one ought, according to my plan, to praise Love with as much eloquence as he can. Let Phaedrus begin first, both because he reclines the first in order, and because he is the father of the discussion."

"No one will vote against you, Eryximachus," said Socrates, "for how can I oppose your proposal, who am ready to confess that I know nothing on any subject but love? *[e]* Or how can Agathon, or Pausanias, or even Aristophanes, whose life is one perpetual ministration to Venus and Bacchus? Or how can any other whom I see here? Though we who sit last are scarcely on an equality with you; for if those who speak before us shall have exhausted the subject with their eloquence and reasonings, our discourses will be superfluous. But in the name of Good Fortune, let Phaedrus begin and praise Love." *[178a]* The

whole party agreed to what Socrates said, and entreated
Phaedrus to begin.

What each then said on this subject, Aristodemus did
not entirely recollect, nor do I recollect all that he related
to me; but only the speeches of those who said what was
most worthy of remembrance. First, then, Phaedrus began
thus: —

"Love is a mighty deity, and the object of admiration,
both to Gods and men, for many and for various claims; but
especially on account of his origin. *[b]* For that he is to be
honoured as one of the most ancient of the Gods, this may
serve as a testimony, that Love has no parents, nor is there
any poet or other person who has ever affirmed that there
are such. Hesiod says, that first 'Chaos was produced; then
the broadbosomed Earth, to be a secure foundation for all
things; then Love.' He says that after Chaos these two were
produced, the Earth and Love. Parmenides, speaking of
generation, says: — 'But he created Love before any of the
Gods.' Acusileus agrees with Hesiod. *[c]* Love, therefore, is
universally acknowledged to be among the eldest of things.
And in addition to this, Love is the author of our greatest
advantages; for I cannot imagine a greater happiness and
advantage to one who is in the flower of youth than an amiable lover, or to a lover than an amiable object of his love.
For neither birth, nor wealth, nor honours, can awaken in
the minds of men the principles which should guide those
who from their youth aspire to an honourable and excellent
life, as Love awakens them. *[d]* I speak of the fear of shame,
which deters them from that which is disgraceful; and the
love of glory which incites to honourable deeds. For it is
not possible that a state or private person should accomplish, without these incitements, anything beautiful or

great. I assert, then, that should one who loves be discovered in any dishonourable action, or tamely enduring insult
through cowardice, *[e]* he would feel more anguish and
shame if observed by the object of his passion, than if he
were observed by his father or his companions, or any other
person. In like manner, one who is the object of love is especially grieved to be discovered by his lover in any dishonourable act. If then, by any contrivance, a state or army
could be composed of lovers* and the beloved, it is beyond
calculation how excellently they would administer their
affairs, refraining from any thing base, *[179a]* contending
with each other for the acquirement of fame, and exhibiting
such valour in battle as that, though few in numbers, they
might subdue all mankind. For should a lover desert the
ranks or cast away his arms in the presence of his beloved,
he would suffer far acuter shame from that one person's
regard, than from the regard of all other men. A thousand
times would he prefer to die, rather than desert the object
of his attachment, and not succour him in danger.

"There is none so worthless whom Love cannot impel,
as it were, by a divine inspiration, towards virtue, even so
that he may through this inspiration become equal to one
who might naturally be more excellent; *[b]* and, in truth, as
Homer says: The God breathes vigour into certain heroes
— so Love breathes into those who love, the spirit which is
produced from himself. Not only men, but even women
who love, are those alone who willingly expose themselves
to die for others. Alcestis, the daughter of Pelias, affords to
the Greeks a remarkable example of this opinion; she alone
being willing to die for her husband, *[c]* and so surpassing
his parents in the affection with which love inspired her
towards him, as to make them appear, in the comparison

with her, strangers to their own child, and related to him
merely in name; and so lovely and admirable did this action
appear, not only to men, but even to the Gods, that,
although they conceded the prerogative of bringing back
the spirit from death to few among the many who then performed excellent and honourable deeds, [d] yet, delighted
with this action, they redeemed her soul from the infernal
regions: so highly do the Gods honour zeal and devotion in
love. They sent back indeed Orpheus, the son of Oeagrus,
from Hell, with his purpose unfulfilled, and, showing him
only the spectre of her for whom he came, refused to render up herself. For Orpheus seemed to them not, as
Alcestis, to have dared die for the sake of her whom he
loved, and thus to secure to himself a perpetual intercourse
with her in the regions to which she had preceded him,* but
like a cowardly musician, to have contrived to descend alive
into Hell; and, indeed, they appointed as a punishment for
his cowardice, that he should be put to death by women.

[e] "Far otherwise did they regard Achilles, the son of
Thetis, whom they sent to inhabit the Islands of the
Blessed. For Achilles, though informed by his mother that
his own death would ensue upon his killing Hector, but that
if he refrained from it he might return home and die in old
age, yet preferred revenging and honouring his beloved
Patroclus; [180a] not to die for him merely, but to disdain
and reject that life which he had ceased to share.*
Therefore the Gods honoured Achilles beyond all other
men, because he thus preferred his friend to all things else.
Aeschylus talks nonsense when he says, that Patroclus was
beloved by Achilles, who was more beautiful, not only than
Patroclus, but than all the other heroes, who was in the
freshness of youth, and beardless, and according to Homer,

much younger than his friend. But in truth the species of
devotion in love which he exhibited is that which the Gods
chiefly honour. *[b]* Far more do they love and admire and
crown with rewards the beloved who cherishes his lover,
than the lover who cherishes his beloved; for the lover is
diviner than the beloved, he is inspired by the God. On this
account have they rewarded Achilles more amply than
Alcestis; permitting his spirit to inhabit the Islands of the
Blessed. Hence do I assert that Love is the most ancient and
venerable of deities, and most powerful to endow mortals
with the possession of happiness and virtue, both whilst
they live and after they die."

[c] Thus Aristodemus reported the discourse of
Phaedrus; and after Phaedrus, he said that some others
spoke, whose discourses he did not well remember. When
they had ceased, Pausanias began thus: —

"Simply to praise Love, O Phaedrus, seems to me too
bounded a scope for our discourse. If Love were one, it
would be well. But since Love is not one, *[d]* I will endeavour to distinguish which is the Love whom it becomes us to
praise, and having thus discriminated one from the other,
will attempt to render him who is the subject of our discourse the honour due to his divinity. We all know that
Venus is never without Love; and if Venus were one, Love
would be one; but since there are two Venuses, of necessity
also must there be two Loves. For assuredly are there two
Venuses; one, the eldest, the daughter of Uranus, born
without a mother, whom we call the Uranian;* *[e]* the other
younger, the daughter of Jupiter and Dione, whom we call
the Pandemian;* — of necessity must there also be two
Loves, the Uranian and Pandemian companions of these
Goddesses. It is becoming to praise all the Gods, but the

attributes which fall to the lot of each may be distinguished and selected. For any particular action whatever, in itself is neither good nor evil; *[181a]* what we are now doing — drinking, singing, talking, none of these things are good in themselves, but the mode in which they are done stamps them with its own nature; and that which is done well, is good, and that which is done ill, is evil. Thus, not all love, nor every mode of love is beautiful, or worthy of commendation, but that alone which excites us to love worthily. The Love, therefore, which attends upon Venus Pandemos is, in truth, common to the vulgar, *[b]* and presides over transient and fortuitous connexions, and is worshipped by the least excellent of mankind: the votaries of this deity regard women as equally objects of love with men; they seek the body rather than the soul, and the ignorant rather than the wise, disdaining all that is honourable and lovely, and considering how they shall best satisfy their sensual necessities. *[c]* This Love is derived from the younger Goddess, who partakes in her nature both of male and female. But the attendant on the other, the Uranian, whose nature is entirely masculine, is the Love who inspires us with affection towards men, and exempts us from all wantonness and libertinism. Those who are inspired by this divinity seek the affections of that sex which is endowed by nature with greater excellence and vigour both of body and mind. And it is easy to distinguish those who especially exist under the influence of this power, *[d]* by their choosing in early youth as the objects of their love those in whom the intellectual faculties have begun to develope: in preference to mere youths. For those who begin to love in this manner, seem to me to be preparing to pass their whole life together in a community of good and evil, and not ever lightly deceiving

those who love them, to be faithless to their vows. There
ought to be a law that none should love mere youths; *[e]* so
much serious affection as this deity enkindles should not be
doubtfully bestowed; for the body and mind of those so
young are yet unformed, and it is difficult to foretell what
will be their future tendencies and power. The good voluntarily impose this law upon themselves, and those vulgar
lovers ought to be compelled to the same observance, as we
deter them with all the power of the laws from the love of
free matrons. *[182a]* For these are persons whose shameful
actions embolden those who observe their importunity and
intemperance, to assert, that it is dishonourable to serve and
gratify the objects of our love. But no one who does this
gracefully and according to law, can justly be liable to the
imputations of blame.

"The law as it relates to love in other cities may be easily understood, for it is plainly defined. *[b]* Here and in
Lacedaemon it is various. In Elis and in Boeotia, where men
are yet unskilled in philosophy and the use of language, the
law simply declares that it is honourable to serve those we
love: nor has any legislator either of ancient or modern
times considered it dishonourable for this reason I imagine,
because unaware of these distinctions, they were unwilling
to throw obstacles in their own way by a vain attempt to dis-
suade the youth wholly from this practice. In Ionia and
many other places, which are subject to the Barbarians, the
law declares this affectionate service to be shameful. *[c]* For
not only this species of love, but philosophy and the practice of the gymnastic exercises, are represented as dishonourable by the tyrannical governments under which the
Barbarians live. For I imagine it would little conduce to the

benefit of the governors, that the governed should be disciplined to lofty thoughts and to unity and communion of
stedfast friendship, of which admirable effects the tyrants of
our own country have also learned that Love is the author.
For the love of Harmodius and Aristogiton,* strengthened
into a firm friendship, dissolved the tyranny. [d] Wherever,
therefore, it is declared dishonourable in any case to serve
and benefit lovers, that law is a mark of the depravity of the
legislator, the avarice and tyranny of the rulers, and the
cowardice of those who are ruled. Wherever it is simply
declared to be honourable without distinction of cases, such
a declaration denotes dulness and want of subtlety of mind
in the authors of the regulation. Here the degrees of praise
or blame to be attributed by law to this practice are far better regulated; but it is yet difficult to determine the cases to
which they should refer.

"It is evident, however, for one in whom this passion is
enkindled, it is more honourable to love openly than
secretly; and most honourable to love the most excellent
and virtuous, even if they should be less beautiful than others. It is honourable for the lover to exhort and sustain the
object of his love in virtuous conduct. [e] It is considered
honourable to attain the love of those whom we seek, and
the contrary shameful; and to facilitate this attainment, the
law has given to the lover the permission of acquiring
favour by the most extraordinary devices, [183a] which if a
person should practise for any purpose besides this, he
would incur the severest reproof of philosophy. For if any
one desirous of accumulating money, or ambitious of
procuring power, or seeking any other advantage, should,
like a lover seeking to acquire the favour of his beloved,

employ prayers and entreaties in his necessity, and swear such oaths as lovers swear, and sleep before the threshold, and offer to subject himself to such slavery as no slave even would endure; he would be frustrated of the attainment of what he sought, both by his enemies and friends; *[b]* these reviling him for his flattery, those sharply admonishing him, and taking to themselves the shame of his servility. But there is a certain grace in a lover who does all these things, and the law declares that he alone may do them without dishonour. It is commonly said that the Gods accord pardon to the lover alone if he should break his oath, and that there is no oath by Venus. *[c]* Thus as our law declares, both Gods and men have given to lovers all possible indulgence.

"Considering these things, how admirable a thing in the state is love, and the affection and the facility of lovers towards each other! But since on the other hand the fathers of those who are the objects of love command their masters* not to suffer them to converse with their lovers, and their comrades reproach them, if they perceive any intimacy of that kind, and those who are old do not reproach the censurers as if they censured unjustly; *[d]* considering these things I say, one might think that this species of service and attachment were held to be dishonourable.

"The affair, however, I imagine, stands thus: As I have before said, Love cannot be considered in itself as either honourable or dishonourable: if it is honourably pursued, it is honourable; if dishonourably, dishonourable: it is dishonourable basely to serve and gratify a worthless person; it is honourable honourably to serve a person of virtue. *[e]* That Pandemic lover who loves rather the body than the soul, is worthless, nor can be constant and consistent, since he has placed his affections on that which has no stability. For as soon as the flower of the form, which was the sole object of his desire, has faded, then he departs and is seen no more; bound by no faith or shame of his many promises and persuasions. But he who is the lover of virtuous manners is constant during life, since he has placed himself in harmony with that which is consistent with itself.

[184a] "The two classes of persons our law directs us to distinguish with careful examination, so that we may serve and converse with the one and avoid the other; determining, by that inquiry, by what the lover is attracted, and for what the object of his love is dear to him. On the same account it is considered dishonourable to be inspired with love at once, lest time should be wanting to know and approve the character of the object. It is considered dishonourable to be captivated by the allurements of wealth and power, *[b]* or terrified through injuries to yield up the affections, or not to despise in the comparison with an unconstrained choice all political influence and personal advantage. For no circumstance is there in wealth or power so invariable and consistent, as that no generous friendship can ever spring up from amongst them. Our law therefore has left one method by which the beloved may gratify his lover. We have a law with respect to lovers which declares that it shall not be considered servile or disgraceful, *[c]* though the lover should submit himself to any species of slavery for the sake of his beloved. The same opinion holds with respect to those who undergo any degradation for the sake of virtue. For it is esteemed among us, that if any one chooses to serve and obey another for the purpose of becoming more wise or more virtuous through the intercourse that might thence arise, such willing slavery is not the slavery of a dishonest flatterer. Through this law we

should consider in the same light a servitude undertaken for the sake of love as one undertaken for the acquirement of wisdom or any other excellence, *[d]* if indeed the devotion of a lover to his beloved is to be considered a beautiful thing. For when the lover and the beloved have once arrived at the same point, the province of each being distinguished; the one serving and gratifying his beloved, now his indeed in all things in which it were not unjust to serve him; the one conceding to his lover, the author of his wisdom and virtue, whatever it were not honourable to refuse; the one able to assist in the cultivation of the mind and in the acquirement of every other excellence; *[e]* the other yet requiring education, and seeking the possession of wisdom; then alone, by the union of these conditions, and in no other case, is it honourable for the beloved to yield up his affections to his lover. In this servitude alone there is no disgrace in being deceived and defeated of the object for which it was undertaken; whereas every other is disgraceful, whether we are deceived or no. *[185a]* For if any one favours his lover for his wealth, and is deceived in the advantage which he expected, his lover turning out to be poor instead of rich, his conduct is not the less base; for such an one has already shown that for the sake of money he would submit in anything to any one. On the same principle, if any one favours another, believing him to be virtuous, for the sake of becoming better through the intercourse and affection for his lover, and is deceived; his lover turning out to be worthless, and far from the possession of virtue; *[b]* yet it is honourable to have been so deceived. For such an one seems to have submitted to the servitude of Love, because he would endure anything from any one for the sake of becoming more virtuous and wise; a disposition of mind eminently beautiful.

"This is that Love who attends on the Uranian deity, and is Uranian; the author of innumerable benefits both to the state and to individuals, and by the necessity of whose influences both the lover and the beloved are disciplined into the zeal of virtue. [c] All other Loves are the attendants on Venus Pandemos. So much, although unpremeditated, is what I have to deliver on the subject of love, O Phaedrus."

Pausanias having ceased (for so the learned teach me to denote the changes of the discourse*), Aristodemus said that it came to the turn of Aristophanes to speak; but that it happened that, from repletion or some other cause, he had an hiccup which prevented him; so he turned to Eryximachus, the physician, who was reclining close beside him, and said — [d] "Eryximachus, it is but fair that you should cure my hiccup, or speak instead of me until it is over." — "I will do both," said Eryximachus; "I will speak in your turn, and you, when your hiccup has ceased, shall speak in mine. Meanwhile, if you hold your breath some time, it will subside. [e] If not, gargle your throat with water; and if it still continues, take something to stimulate your nostrils, and sneeze; do this once or twice, and even though it should be very violent it will cease." — "Whilst you speak," said Aristophanes, "I will follow your directions." — Eryximachus then began: —

[186a] "Since Pausanias, beginning his discourse excellently, placed no fit completion and developement to it, I think it necessary to attempt to fill up what he has left unfinished. He has reasoned well in defining Love as of a

double nature. The science of medicine, to which I have
addicted myself, seems to teach me that the love which
impels towards those who are beautiful, does not subsist
only in the souls of men, but in the bodies also of those of
all other living beings which are produced upon earth, and,
in a word, in all things which are. *[b]* So wonderful and
mighty is this divinity, and so widely is his influence extend-
ed over all divine and human things! For the honour of my
profession, I will begin by adducing a proof from medicine.
The nature of the body contains within itself this double
Love. For that which is healthy and that which is diseased
in a body differ and are unlike: that which is unlike, loves
and desires that which is unlike. Love, therefore, is different
in a sane and in a diseased body. Pausanias has asserted
rightly that it is honourable to gratify those things in the
body which are good and healthy, *[c]* and in this consists the
skill of the physician; whilst those which are bad and diseased, ought to be treated with no indulgence. The science
of medicine, in a word, is a knowledge of the love affairs of
the body, as they bear relation to repletion and evacuation;
[d] and he is the most skilful physician who can trace in
those operations the good and evil love, can make the one
change places with the other, and attract love into those
parts from which he is absent, or expel him from those
which he ought not to occupy. He ought to make those
things which are most inimical, friendly, and excite them to
mutual love. But those things are most inimical, which are
most opposite to each other: cold to heat, bitterness to
sweetness, dryness to moisture. *[e]* Our progenitor,
Aesculapius, as the poets inform us, (and indeed I believe
them,) thro' the skill which he possessed to inspire Love and

concord in these contending principles, established the science of medicine.

"The gymnastic arts and agriculture, no less than medicine, are exercised under the dominion of this God. *[187a]* Music, as any one may perceive who yields a very slight attention to the subject, originates from the same source; which Heraclitus probably meant, though he could not express his meaning very clearly in words, when he says, 'One though apparently differing, yet so agrees with itself, as the harmony of a lyre and a bow.' It is great absurdity to say that an harmony differs, and can exist between things whilst they are dissimilar; *[b]* but probably he meant that from sounds which first differed, like the grave and the acute, and which afterwards agreed, harmony was produced according to musical art. For no harmony can arise from the grave and the acute whilst yet they differ. But harmony is symphony: symphony is, as it were, concord. But it is impossible that concord should subsist between things that differ, so long as they differ. Between things which are discordant and dissimilar there is then no harmony. *[c]* A rhythm is produced from that which is quick, and that which is slow, first being distinguished and opposed to each other, and then made accordant; so does medicine, no less than music, establish a concord between the objects of its art, producing love and agreement between adverse things.

"Music is then the knowledge of that which relates to Love in harmony and rhythm. In the very system of harmony and rhythm, it is easy to distinguish love. The double Love is not distinguishable in music itself; *[d]* but it is required to apply it to the service of mankind by rhythm and harmony, which is called poetry, or the composition of melody; or by the correct use of songs and measures already composed, which is called discipline; then one can be distinguished from the other, by the aid of an extremely skilful artist.* And the better love ought to be honoured and preserved for the sake of those who are virtuous, and that the nature of the vicious may be changed through the inspiration of its spirit. *[e]* This is that beautiful Uranian love, the attendant of the Uranian muse: the Pandemian is the attendant of Polymnia;* to whose influence we should only so far subject ourselves, as to derive pleasure from it without indulging to excess; in the same manner as, according to our art, we are instructed to seek the pleasures of the table, only so far as we can enjoy them without the consequences of disease. In music, therefore, and in medicine, and in all other things, human and divine, this double Love ought to be traced and discriminated; for it is in all things.

[188a] "Even the constitution of the seasons of the year is penetrated with these contending principles. For so often as heat and cold, dryness and moisture, of which I spoke before, are influenced by the more benignant Love, and are harmoniously and temperately intermingled with the seasons, they bring maturity and health to men, and to all other animals and plants. But when the evil and injurious Love assumes the dominion of the seasons of the year, destruction is spread widely abroad. *[b]* Then pestilence is accustomed to arise, and many other blights and diseases fall upon animals and plants: and hoar frosts, and hails, and mildew on the corn, are produced from that excessive and disorderly love, with which each season of the year is impelled towards the other; the motions of which and the knowledge of the stars, is called astronomy. *[c]* All sacrifices, and all those things in which divination is concerned (for

these things are the links by which is maintained an intercourse and communion between the Gods and men) are
nothing else than the science of preservation and right government of Love. For impiety is accustomed to spring up,
so soon as any one ceases to serve the more honourable
Love, and worship him by the sacrifice of good actions; but
submits himself to the influences of the other, in relation of
his duties towards his parents, and the Gods, and the living,
and the dead. It is the object of divination to distinguish
and remedy the effects of these opposite Loves; [d] and divination is therefore the author of the friendship of Gods
and men, because it affords the knowledge of what in matters of Love is lawful or unlawful to men.

"Thus every species of Love possesses collectively a
various and vast, or rather universal power. But Love which
incites to the acquirement of its objects according to virtue
and wisdom, possesses the most exclusive dominion, and
prepares for his worshippers the highest happiness through
the mutual intercourse of social kindness which it promotes
among them, and through the benevolence which he
attracts to them from the Gods, our superiors.

[e] "Probably in thus praising Love, I have unwillingly
omitted many things; but it is your business, O
Aristophanes, to fill up all that I have left incomplete; or, if
you have imagined any other mode of honouring the divinity; for I observe your hiccup is over."

[189a] "Yes," said Aristophanes, "but not before I
applied the sneezing. I wonder why the harmonious con-
struction of our body should require such noisy operations
as sneezing; for it ceased the moment I sneezed." — "Do
you not observe what you do, my good Aristophanes?" said
Eryximachus; "you are going to speak, and you predispose

us to laughter, *[b]* and compel me to watch for the first ridiculous idea which you may start in your discourse, when you might have spoken in peace." — "Let me unsay what I have said, then," replied Aristophanes, laughing. "Do not watch me, I entreat you; though I am not afraid of saying what is laughable (since that would be all gain, and quite in the accustomed spirit of my muse) but lest I should say what is ridiculous." — "Do you think to throw your dart, and escape with impunity, Aristophanes? Attend, and what you say be careful you maintain; *[c]* then, perhaps, if it pleases me, I may dismiss you without question."

"Indeed, Eryximachus," proceeded Aristophanes, "I have designed that my discourse should be very different from yours and that of Pausanias. It seems to me that mankind are by no means penetrated with a conception of the power of Love, or they would have built sumptuous temples and altars, and have established magnificent rites of sacrifice in his honour; he deserves worship and homage more than all the other Gods, and he has yet received none. *[d]* For Love is of all the Gods the most friendly to mortals; and the physician of those wounds, whose cure would be the greatest happiness which could be conferred upon the human race. I will endeavour to unfold to you his true power, and you can relate what I declare to others.

"You ought first to know the nature of man, and the adventures he has gone through; for his nature was anciently far different from that which it is at present. First, then, human beings were formerly not divided into two sexes, male and female; *[e]* there was also a third, common to both the others, the name of which remains, though the sex itself has disappeared. The androgynous sex, both in appearance and in name, was common both to male and female; its name alone remains, which labours under a reproach.

"At the period to which I refer, the form of every human being was round, the back and the sides being circularly joined, and each had four arms and as many legs; *[190a]* two faces fixed upon a round neck, exactly like each other; one head between the two faces; four ears, and two organs of generation; and everything else as from such proportions it is easy to conjecture. Man walked upright as now, in whatever direction he pleased; and when he wished to go fast he made use of all his eight limbs, and proceeded in a rapid motion by rolling circularly round, — like tumblers, who, with their legs in the air, tumble round and round. *[b]* We account for the production of three sexes by supposing that, at the beginning, the male was produced from the Sun, the female from the Earth; and that sex which participated in both sexes, from the Moon, by reason of the androgynous nature of the Moon. They were round, and their mode of proceeding was round, from the similarity which must needs subsist between them and their parent.

"They were strong also, and had aspiring thoughts. They it was who levied war against the Gods; and what Homer writes concerning Ephialtes and Otus,* that they sought to ascend heaven and dethrone the Gods, in reality relates to this primitive people. *[c]* Jupiter and the other Gods debated what was to be done in this emergency. For neither could they prevail on themselves to destroy them, as they had the Giants, with thunder, so that the race should be abolished; for in that case they would be deprived of the honours of the sacrifices which they were in the custom of receiving from them; nor could they permit a continuance of their insolence and impiety. Jupiter, with some difficulty having devised a scheme, at length spoke. 'I think,' said he, 'I have contrived a method by which we may, *[d]* by rendering the human race more feeble, quell the insolence which they exercise, without proceeding to their utter destruction. I will cut each of them in half; and so they will at once be weaker and more useful on account of their numbers. They shall walk upright on two legs. If they show any more insolence, and will not keep quiet, I will cut them up in half again, so they shall go about hopping on one leg.'

[e] "So saying, he cut human beings in half, as people cut eggs before they salt them, or as I have seen eggs cut with hairs. He ordered Apollo to take each one as he cut him, and turn his face and half his neck towards the operation, so that by contemplating it he might become more cautious and humble; and then to cure him, Apollo turned the face round, and drawing the skin upon what we now call the belly, like a contracted pouch, and leaving one opening, that which is called the navel, tied it in the middle. *[191a]* He then smoothed many other wrinkles, and moulded the breast with much such an instrument as the leather-cutters use to smooth the skins upon the block. He left only a few wrinkles in the belly, near the navel, to serve as a record of its former adventure. Immediately after this division, as each desired to possess the other half of himself, these divided people threw their arms around and embraced each other, seeking to grow together; and from this resolution to do nothing without the other half, they died of hunger and weakness: *[b]* when one half died and the other was left alive, that which was thus left sought another and folded it to its bosom; whether that half were an entire woman (for we now

call it a woman) or a man; and thus they perished. But
Jupiter, pitying them, thought of another contrivance, and
placed the parts of generation before. [c] Since formerly
when these parts were exposed they produced their kind
not by the assistance of each other, but like grasshoppers,
by engendering upon the earth. In this manner is generation now produced, by the union of male and female; so
that from the embrace of a man and woman the race is
propagated, but from those of the same sex no such consequence ensues.*

[d] "From this period, mutual Love has naturally existed in human beings; that reconciler and bond of union of
their original nature, which seeks to make two, one, and to
heal the divided nature of man. Every one of us is thus the
half of what may be properly termed a man, and like a flatfish* cut in two, is the imperfect portion of an entire whole,
perpetually necessitated to seek the half belonging to him.
Those who are a section of what was formerly one man and
woman, are lovers of the female sex, and most of the adul-
terers, [e] and those women who fall in love with men and
intrigue with them, belong to this species. Those women
who are a section of what in its unity contained two women,
are not much attracted by the male sex, but have their incli-
nations principally engaged by their own. And those who
become adulteresses with female partners* belong to this
division. Those who are a section of what in the beginning
was entirely male seek the society of males; and before they
arrive at manhood, such being portions of what was masculine, are delighted with the intercourse and familiarity of
men. [192a] These are the youths who, being of a more
manly nature, promise the fairest harvest of future excellence. Some attach to them the reproach of libertinism and

immodesty, but without justice; for they do not seek an intercourse with men from any immodesty but from the impulses of a generous, aspiring and manly nature. A great proof of which is that such alone ever attain to political power.* *[b]* When they arrive at manhood they still only associate with those of their own sex; and they never engage in marriage and the propagation of the species from sensual desire but only in obedience to the laws. It would be sufficient to them if they lived for ever unmarried in the mutual society of their equals.

"Such as I have described is ever an affectionate lover and a faithful friend, delighting in that which is in conformity with his own nature. *[c]* Whenever, therefore, any such as I have described are impetuously struck, through the sentiment of their former union, with love and desire and the want of community, they are ever unwilling to be divided even for a moment. These are they who devote their whole lives to each other, with a vain and inexpressible longing to obtain from each other something they know not what; for it is not merely the sensual delights* of their intercourse for the sake of which they dedicate themselves to each with such serious affection; *[d]* but the soul of each manifestly thirsts for, from the other, something which there are no words to describe, and divines that which it seeks, and traces obscurely the footsteps of its obscure desire.* If Vulcan should stand over the couch of these persons thus affected as they were reclining together, with his tools, and should say to them, 'My good people, what is it that you want with one another?' And if, while they were hesitating what to answer, he should proceed to ask, 'Do you not desire the closest union and singleness to exist between you, so that you may never be divided night or day? *[e]* If so, I will melt you together, and make you grow into one, so that both in life and death ye may be undivided. Consider, is this what you desire? Will it content you if you become that which I propose?' We all know that no one would refuse such an offer, but would at once feel that this was what he had ever sought; and intimately to mix and melt and to be melted together with his beloved, so that one should be made out of two.

"The cause of this desire is, that according to our original nature, we were once entire. *[193a]* The desire and the pursuit of integrity and union is that which we all love. First, as I said, we were entire, but now we have been divided through our own wickedness, as the Arcadians by the Lacedaemonians. There is reason to fear, if we are guilty of any additional impiety towards the Gods, *[b]* that we may be cut in two again, and may go about like those figures painted on the columns, divided through the middle of our nostrils, as thin as halved dice.* On which account every man ought to be exhorted to pay due reverence to the Gods, that we may escape so severe a punishment, and obtain those things which Love, our general and commander, incites us to desire; against whom let none rebel by exciting the hatred of the Gods. For if we continue on good terms with them, we may discover and possess those lost and concealed objects of our love; a good-fortune which now befalls to few. Nor let Eryximachus take up that expression as if I alluded to Pausanias and Agathon; *[c]* for though probably they, who are manly by nature, are to be ranked among those fortunate few, I assert that the happiness of all, both men and women, consists singly in the fulfilment of their Love, and in that possession of its objects by which we are in some degree restored to our antient nature. If this be the completion of felicity, that must necessarily approach nearest to it, in which we obtain the possession and society of those whose natures most intimately accord with our own. And if we would celebrate any God as the author of this benefit, *[d]* we should justly celebrate Love with hymns of joy; who, in our present condition, brings good assistance in our necessity, and affords great hopes, if we persevere in piety towards the Gods, that he will restore us to our original state, and confer on us the complete happiness alone suited to our nature.

"Such, Eryximachus, is my discourse on the subject of Love; different indeed from yours, which I nevertheless entreat you not to turn into ridicule, *[e]* that we may not interrupt what each has separately to deliver on the subject."

"I will refrain at present," said Eryximachus, "for your discourse delighted me. And if I did not know that Socrates and Agathon were profoundly versed in the science of love affairs, I should fear that they had nothing new to say, after so many and such various imaginations. *[194a]* As it is, I confide in the fertility of their geniuses."* — "Your part of the contest, at least, was strenuously fought, Eryximachus," said Socrates, "but if you had been in the situation in which I am, or rather shall be, after the discourse of Agathon, like me, you would then have reason to fear, and be reduced to your wits' end." — "Socrates," said Agathon, "wishes to confuse me with the enchantments of his wit, sufficiently confused already with the expectation I see in the assembly in favour of my discourse." — "I must have lost my memory, Agathon," replied Socrates, *[b]* "if I imagined that you could be disturbed by a few private persons, after having witnessed your firmness and courage in ascending the rostrum with the actors, and in calmly reciting your compositions in the presence of so great an assembly as that which decreed you the prize of tragedy." — "What then, Socrates," retorted Agathon, "do you think me so full of the theatre as to be ignorant that the judgement of a few wise is more awful than that of a multitude of others, to one who rightly balances the value of their suffrages?" — [c] "I should judge ill indeed, Agathon," answered Socrates, "in thinking you capable of any rude and unrefined conception, for I well know that if you meet with any whom you consider wise, you esteem such alone of more value than all others. But we are far from being entitled to this distinction, for we were also of that assembly, and to be numbered among the rest. But should you meet with any who are really wise, you would be careful to say nothing in their presence which you thought they would not approve — is it not so?" — "Certainly," replied Agathon. — "You would not then exercise the same caution in the presence of the multitude in which they were included?" — [d] "My dear Agathon," said Phaedrus, interrupting him, "if you answer all the questions of Socrates, they will never have an end; he will urge them without conscience so long as he can get any person, especially one who is so beautiful, to dispute with him. I own it delights me to hear Socrates discuss; but at present, I must see that Love is not defrauded of the praise which it is my province to exact from each of you. Pay the God his due, and then reason between yourselves if you will."

[e] "Your admonition is just, Phaedrus," replied Agathon, "nor need any reasoning I hold with Socrates impede me; we shall find many future opportunities for

discussion. I will begin my discourse then, first having
defined what ought to be the subject of it. All who have
already spoken seem to me not so much to have praised
Love, as to have felicitated mankind on the many advantages of which that deity is the cause; *[195a]* what he is, the
author of these great benefits, none have yet declared.
There is one mode alone of celebration which would comprehend the whole topic, namely, first to declare what are
those benefits, and then what he is who is the author of
those benefits, which are the subject of our discourse. Love
ought first to be praised, and then his gifts declared. I assert,
then, that although all the Gods are immortally happy,
Love, if I dare trust my voice to express so awful a truth, is
the happiest, and most excellent, and the most beautiful.
That he is the most beautiful is evident; *[b]* first, O
Phaedrus, from this circumstance, that he is the youngest of
the Gods; and, secondly, from his fleetness, and his repugnance to all that is old; for he escapes with the swiftness of
wings from old age; a thing in itself sufficiently swift, since
it overtakes us sooner than there is need; and which Love,
who delights in the intercourse of the young, hates, and in
no manner can be induced to enter into community with.
The ancient proverb, which says that like is attracted by
like, applies to the attributes of Love. I concede many
things to you, O Phaedrus, but this I do not concede, that
Love is more ancient than Saturn and Japetus.* *[c]* I assert
that he is not only the youngest of the Gods, but invested
with everlasting youth. Those ancient deeds among the
Gods recorded by Hesiod and Parmenides, if their relations
are to be considered as true, were produced not by Love,
but by Necessity. For if Love had been then in Heaven,
those violent and sanguinary crimes never would have taken

place; but there would ever have subsisted that affection and peace, in which the Gods now live, under the influence of Love.

"He is young, therefore, and being young is tender and soft. *[d]* There were need of some poet like Homer to celebrate the delicacy and tenderness of Love. For Homer says, that the Goddess Calamity is delicate, and that her feet are tender. 'Her feet are soft,' he says, 'for she treads not upon the ground, but makes her path upon the heads of men.' He gives as an evidence of her tenderness, that she walks not upon that which is hard, but that which is soft. *[e]* The same evidence is sufficient to make manifest the tenderness of Love. For Love walks not upon the earth, nor over the heads of men, which are not indeed very soft; but he dwells within, and treads on the softest of existing things, having established his habitation within the souls and inmost nature of Gods and men; not indeed in all souls — for wherever he chances to find a hard and rugged disposition, there he will not inhabit, but only where it is most soft and tender. *[196a]* Of needs must he be the most delicate of all things, who touches lightly with his feet only the softest parts of those things which are the softest of all.

"He is then the youngest and the most delicate of all divinities; and in addition to this, he is, as it were, the most moist and liquid. For if he were otherwise, he could not, as he does, fold himself around everything, and secretly flow out and into every soul. His loveliness, that which Love possesses far beyond all other things, is a manifestation of the liquid and flowing symmetry of his form; for between deformity and Love there is eternal contrast and repugnance. His life is spent among flowers, and this accounts for the immortal fairness of his skin; *[b]* for the winged Love rests not in his flight on any form, or within any soul the flower of whose loveliness is faded, but there remains most willingly where is the odour and radiance of blossoms, yet unwithered. Concerning the beauty of the God, let this be sufficient, though many things must remain unsaid. Let us next consider the virtue and power of Love.

"What is most admirable in Love is, that he neither inflicts nor endures injury in his relations either with Gods or men. Nor if he suffers any thing does he suffer it through violence, [c] nor doing anything does he act it with violence, for Love is never even touched with violence. Every one willingly administers every thing to Love; and that which every one voluntarily concedes to another, the laws, which are the kings of the republic, decree that it is just for him to possess. In addition to justice, Love participates in the highest temperance; for if temperance is defined to be the being superior to and holding under dominion pleasures and desires; then Love, than whom no pleasure is more powerful, and who is thus more powerful than all persuasions and delights, must be excellently temperate. [d] In power and valour Mars cannot contend with Love: the love of Venus possesses Mars; the possessor is always superior to the possessed, and he who subdues the most powerful must of necessity be the most powerful of all.

"The justice and temperance and valour of the God have been thus declared; — there remains to exhibit his wisdom. [e] And first, that, like Eryximachus, I may honour my own profession, the God is a wise poet; so wise that he can even make a poet one who was not before: for every one, even if before he were ever so undisciplined, becomes a poet as soon as he is touched by Love; a sufficient proof that

Love is a great poet, and well skilled in that science according to the discipline of music. For what any one possesses not, or knows not, that can he neither give nor teach another. *[197a]* And who will claim that the divine poetry, by which all living things are produced upon the earth, is harmonized by the wisdom of Love? Is it not evident that Love was the author of all the arts of life with which we are acquainted, and that he whose teacher has been Love, becomes eminent and illustrious, whilst he who knows not Love, remains forever unregarded and obscure? Apollo invented medicine, and divination, and archery, under the guidance of desire and Love; *[b]* so that Apollo was the disciple of Love. Through him the Muses discovered the arts of literature, and Vulcan that of moulding brass, and Minerva the loom, and Jupiter the mystery of the dominion which he now exercises over Gods and men. So were the Gods taught and disciplined by the love of that which is beautiful; for there is no love towards deformity.

"At the origin of things, as I have before said, many fearful deeds are reported to have been done among the Gods, on account of the dominion of Necessity. But so soon as this deity sprang forth from the desire which forever tends in the Universe towards that which is lovely, then all blessings descended upon all living things, human and divine. *[c]* Love seems to me, O Phaedrus, a divinity the most beautiful and the best of all, and the author to all others of the excellencies with which his own nature is endowed. Nor can I restrain the poetic enthusiasm which takes possession of my discourse, and bids me declare that Love is the divinity who creates peace among men, and calm upon the sea, the windless silence of storms, repose and sleep in sadness. *[d]* Love divests us of all alienation from each other, and fills our vacant hearts with overflowing sympathy;* he gathers us together in such social meetings as we now delight to celebrate, our guardian and our guide in dances, and sacrifices, and feasts. Yes, Love who showers benignity upon the world, and before whose presence all harsh passions flee and perish; the author of all soft affections; the destroyer of all ungentle thoughts; merciful, mild; the object of the admiration of the wise, and the delight of Gods; possessed by the fortunate, and desired by the unhappy, therefore unhappy because they possess him not; the father of grace, and delicacy, and gentleness, and delight, and persuasion, and desire; the cherisher of all that is good, the abolisher of all evil; *[e]* our most excellent pilot, defence, saviour and guardian in labour and in fear, in desire and in reason; the ornament and governor of all things human and divine; the best, the loveliest; in whose footsteps everyone ought to follow, celebrating him excellently in song, and bearing each his part in that divinest harmony which Love sings to all things which live and are, soothing the troubled minds of Gods and men. This, O Phaedrus, is what I have to offer in praise of the Divinity; partly composed, indeed, of thoughtless and playful fancies, and partly of such serious ones, as I could well command."

[198a] No sooner had Agathon ceased, than a loud murmur of applause arose from all present; so becomingly had the fair youth spoken, both in praise of the God, and in extenuation of himself. Then Socrates, addressing Eryximachus, said, "Was not my fear reasonable, son of Acumenus? Did I not divine what has, in fact, happened, — that Agathon's discourse would be so wonderfully beautiful, as to pre-occupy all interest in what I should say?" — "You,

indeed, divined well so far, O Socrates," said Eryximachus, "that Agathon would speak eloquently, but not that, therefore, you would be reduced to any difficulty." — *[b]* "How, my good friend, can I or any one else be otherwise than reduced to difficulty, who speak after a discourse so various and so eloquent, and which otherwise had been sufficiently wonderful, if, at the conclusion, the splendour of the sentences, and the choice selection of the expressions, had not struck all the hearers with astonishment; *[c]* so that I, who well know that I can never say anything nearly so beautiful as this, would, if there had been any escape, have run away for shame. The story of Gorgias came into my mind, and I was afraid lest in reality I should suffer what Homer describes; and lest Agathon, scaring my discourse with the head of the eloquent Gorgias,* should turn me to stone for speechlessness. *[d]* I immediately perceived how ridiculously I had engaged myself with you to assume a part in rendering praise to Love, and had boasted that I was well skilled in amatory matters, being so ignorant of the manner in which it is becoming to render him honour, as I now perceive myself to be. I, in my simplicity, imagined that the truth ought to be spoken concerning each of the topics of our praise, and that it would be sufficient, choosing those which are the most honourable to the God, to place them in as luminous an arrangement as we could. I had, therefore, great hopes that I should speak satisfactorily, being well aware that I was acquainted with the true foundations of the praise which we have engaged to render. *[e]* But since, as it appears, that our purpose has been, not to render Love his due honour, but to accumulate the most beautiful and the greatest attributes of his divinity, whether they in truth belong to it or not, and that the proposed question is not how Love ought to be praised, but how we should praise him most eloquently, my attempt must of necessity fail. It is on this account, I imagine, that in your discourses you have attributed everything to Love, *[199a]* and have described him to be the author of such and so great effects as, to those who are ignorant of his true nature, may exhibit him as the most beautiful and the best of all things. Not, indeed, to those who know the truth. Such praise has a splendid and imposing effect, but as I am unacquainted with the art of rendering it, my mind, which could not foresee what would be required of me, absolves me from that which my tongue promised. Farewell, then, for such praise I can never render.

[b] "But if you desire, I will speak what I feel to be true; and that I may not expose myself to ridicule, I entreat you to consider that I speak without entering into competition with those who have preceded me. Consider, then, Phaedrus, whether you will exact from me such a discourse, containing the mere truth with respect to Love, and composed of such unpremeditated expressions as may chance to offer themselves to my mind." — Phaedrus and the rest bade him speak in the manner which he judged most befitting. — "Permit me, then, O Phaedrus, to ask Agathon a few questions, so that, confirmed by his agreement with me, I may proceed." — *[c]* "Willingly," replied Phaedrus, "ask." — Then Socrates thus began: —

"I applaud, dear Agathon, the beginning of your discourse, where you say, we ought first to define and declare what Love is, and then his works. This rule I particularly approve. But, come, since you have given us a discourse of such beauty and majesty concerning Love, you are able, I doubt not, *[d]* to explain this question, whether Love is the

Love of something or nothing? I do not ask you of what parents Love is; for the enquiry, of whether Love is the love of any father or mother, would be sufficiently ridiculous. But if I were asking you to describe that which a father is, I should ask, not whether a father was the love of any one, but whether a father was the father of any one or not; you would undoubtedly reply, that a father was the father of a son or daughter; would you not?" — "Assuredly." — "You would define a mother in the same manner?" — "Without doubt." — *[e]* "Yet bear with me, and answer a few more questions, for I would learn from you that which I wish to know. If I should enquire, in addition, is not a brother, through the very nature of his relation, the brother of some one?" — "Certainly." — "Of a brother or sister is he not?" — "Without question." — "Try to explain to me then the nature of Love; Love is the love of something or nothing?" — "Of something, certainly."

[200a] "Observe and remember this concession. Tell me yet farther, whether Love desires that of which it is the Love or not?" — "It desires it, assuredly." — "Whether possessing that which it desires and loves, or not possessing it, does it desire and love?" — "Not possessing it, I should imagine." — "Observe now, whether it does not appear, that, of necessity, desire desires that which it wants and does not possess, *[b]* and no longer desires that which it no longer wants: this appears to me, Agathon, of necessity to be; how does it appear to you?" — "It appears so to me also." — "Would any one who was already illustrious, desire to be illustrious; would any one already strong, desire to be strong?" — "From what has already been conceded, it follows that he would not." — "If any one already strong, should desire to be strong; or any one already swift,

should desire to be swift; or any one already healthy, should desire to be healthy, *[c]* it must be concluded that they still desired the advantages of what they already seemed possessed. To destroy the foundation of this error, observe, Agathon, that each of these persons must possess the several advantages in question, at the moment present to our thoughts, whether he will or no. And, now, is it possible that those advantages should be at that time the objects of his desire? For, if any one should say, being in health, 'I desire to be in health'; being rich, 'I desire to be rich, and thus still desire those things which I already possess,' we might say to him, *[d]* 'You, my friend, possess health, and strength, and riches; you do not desire to possess now, but to continue to possess them in future; for, whether you will or no, they now belong to you. Consider then, whether, when you say that you desire things present to you, and in your own possession, you say anything else than that you desire the advantages to be for the future also in your possession.' What else could he reply?" — "Nothing, indeed." — "Is not Love, then, the love of that which is not within its reach, and which cannot hold in security, for the future, those things of which it obtains a present and transitory possession?" — *[e]* "Evidently." — "Love, therefore, and every thing else that desires anything, desires that which is absent and beyond his reach, that which it has not, that which is not itself, that which it wants; such are the things of which there are desire and love." — "Assuredly."

"Come," said Socrates, "let us review your concessions. Is Love anything else than the love first of something; and, secondly, of those things of which it has need?" — *[201a]* "Nothing." — "Now, remember of those things you said in your discourse, that Love was the love — if you wish I will remind you. I think you said something of this kind, that all the affairs of the Gods were admirably disposed through the love of the things which are beautiful; for there was no love of things deformed; did you not say so?" — "I confess that I did." — "You said what was most likely to be true, my friend; and if the matter be so, the love of beauty must be one thing, and the love of deformity another." — "Certainly." — *[b]* "It is conceded, then, that Love loves that which he wants but possesses not?" — "Yes, certainly." — "But Love wants and does not possess beauty?" — "Indeed it must necessarily follow." — "What, then! call you that beautiful which has need of beauty and possesses not?" — "Assuredly no." — "Do you still assert, then, that Love is beautiful, if all that we have said be true?" — "Indeed, Socrates," said Agathon, "I am in danger of being convicted of ignorance, with respect to all that I then spoke." — *[c]* "You spoke most eloquently, my dear Agathon; but bear with my questions yet a moment. You admit that things which are good are also beautiful?" — "No doubt." — "If Love, then, be in want of beautiful things, and things which are good are beautiful, he must be in want of things which are good?" — "I cannot refute your arguments, Socrates." — "You cannot refute truth, my dear Agathon: to refute Socrates is nothing difficult.

[d] "But I will dismiss these questionings. At present let me endeavour, to the best of my power, to repeat to you, on the basis of the points which have been agreed upon between me and Agathon, a discourse concerning Love, which I formerly heard from the prophetess* Diotima, who was profoundly skilled in this and many other doctrines, and who, ten years before the pestilence,* procured to the Athenians, through their sacrifices, a delay of the disease;

for it was she who taught me the science of things relating
to Love.

[e] "As you well remarked, Agathon, we ought to declare
who and what is Love, and then his works. It is easiest to
relate them in the same order, as the foreign prophetess
observed when, questioning me, she related them. For I said
to her much the same things that Agathon has just said to
me — that Love was a great deity, and that he was beautiful; and she refuted me with the same reasons as I have
employed to refute Agathon, compelling me to infer that he
was neither beautiful or good, as I said — 'What then,' I
objected, 'O Diotima, is Love ugly and evil?' — 'Good
words, I entreat you,' said Diotima; 'do you think that every
thing which is not beautiful, must of necessity be ugly?' —
[202a] 'Certainly.' — 'And every thing that is not wise,
ignorant? Do you not perceive that there is something
between ignorance and wisdom?' — 'What is that?' — 'To
have a right opinion or conjecture. Observe, that this kind
of opinion, for which no reason can be rendered, cannot be
called knowledge; for how can that be called knowledge,
which is without evidence or reason? Nor ignorance, on the
other hand; for how can that be called ignorance which
arrives at the persuasion of that which really is? A right
opinion is something between understanding and ignorance.' — I confessed that what she alledged was true. — *[b]*
'Do not then say,' she continued, 'that what is not beautiful
is of necessity deformed, nor what is not good is of necessity evil; nor, since you have confessed that Love is neither
beautiful or good, infer, therefore, that he is deformed or
evil, but rather something intermediate.'

"'But,' I said, 'Love is confessed by all to be a great
God.' — 'Do you mean, when you say all, all those who

know, or those who know not, what they say?' — 'All collectively.' — 'And how can that be, Socrates?' said she laughing; [c] 'how can he be acknowledged to be a great God, by those who assert that he is not even a God at all?' — 'And who are they?' I said. — 'You for one, and I for another.' — 'How can you say that, Diotima?' — 'Easily,' she replied, 'and with truth; for tell me, do you not own that all the Gods are beautiful and happy? or will you presume to maintain that any God is otherwise?' — 'By Jupiter, not I!' — 'Do you not call those alone happy who possess all things that are beautiful and good?' — 'Certainly.' — [d] 'You have confessed that Love, through his desire for things beautiful and good, possesses not those materials of happiness.' — 'Indeed such was my concession.' — 'But how can we conceive a God to be without the possession of what is beautiful and good?' — 'In no manner, I confess.' — 'Observe, then, that you do not consider Love to be a God.' — 'What then,' I said, 'is love a mortal?' — 'By no means.' — 'But what, then?' — 'Like those things which I have before instanced, he is neither mortal or immortal, but something intermediate.' — 'What is that, O Diotima?' — [e] 'A great Daemon, Socrates; and every thing daemoniacal holds an intermediate place between what is divine and what is mortal.'

"'What is his power and nature?' I inquired. — 'He interprets and makes a communication between divine and human things, conveying the prayers and sacrifices of men to the Gods, and communicating the commands and directions concerning the mode of worship most pleasing to them, from Gods to men. He fills up that intermediate space between these two classes of beings, so as to bind together, by his own power, the whole universe of things.

Through him subsist all divination, and the science of
sacred things as it relates to sacrifices, and expiations, and
disenchantments, and prophecy, and magic. *[203a]* The
divine nature cannot immediately communicate with what
is human, but all that intercourse and converse which is
conceded by the Gods to men, both whilst they sleep and
when they wake, subsists through the intervention of Love;
and he who is wise in the science of this intercourse is
supremely happy, and participates in the daemoniacal
nature; whilst he who is wise in any other science or art,
remains a mere ordinary slave. These daemons are, indeed,
many and various, and one of them is Love.'

"'Who are the parents of Love?' I enquired. — *[b]* 'The
history of what you ask,' replied Diotima, 'is somewhat
long; nevertheless I will explain it to you. On the birth of
Venus the Gods celebrated a great feast, and among them
Plenty, the son of Metis.* After supper, Poverty, observing
the profusion, came to beg, and stood beside the door.
Plenty being drunk with nectar, for wine was not yet invented, went out into Jupiter's garden, and fell into a deep sleep.
Poverty wishing to have a child by Plenty, on account of her
low estate, *[c]* lay down by him, and from his embraces conceived Love. Love is, therefore, the follower and servant of
Venus, because he was conceived at her birth, and because
by nature he is a lover of all that is beautiful, and Venus was
beautiful. And since Love is the child of Poverty and Plenty,
his nature and fortune participates in that of his parents. He
is for ever poor, and so far from being delicate and beautiful, as mankind imagine, *[d]* he is squalid and withered; he
flies low along the ground, and is homeless and unsandalled;
he sleeps without covering before the doors, and in the
unsheltered streets; possessing thus far his mother's nature,

that he is ever the companion of Want. But, inasmuch as he participates in that of his father, he is for ever scheming to obtain things which are good and beautiful; he is fearless, vehement, and strong; a dreadful hunter, for ever weaving some new contrivance; exceedingly cautious and prudent, and full of resources; he is also, during his whole existence, a philosopher,* a powerful enchanter, a wizard, and a subtle sophist. *[e]* And, as his nature is neither mortal nor immortal, on the same day when he is fortunate and successful, he will at one time flourish, and then die away, and then, according to his father's nature, again revive. All that he acquires perpetually flows away from him, so that Love is never either rich or poor, and holding for ever an intermediate state between ignorance and wisdom. *[204a]* The case stands thus — no God philosophizes or desires to become wise, for he is wise; nor, if there exist any other being who is wise, does he philosophize. Nor do the ignorant philosophize, for they desire not to become wise; for this is the evil of ignorance, that he who has neither intelligence, nor virtue, nor delicacy of sentiment, imagines that he possesses all those things sufficiently. He seeks not, therefore, that possession of whose want they are not aware.' — 'Who, then, O Diotima,' I enquired, 'are philosophers, if they are neither the ignorant nor the wise?' — *[b]* 'It is evident, even to a child, that they are those intermediate persons, among whom is Love. For Wisdom is one of the most beautiful of all things; Love is that which thirsts for the beautiful, so that Love is of necessity a philosopher, philosophy being an intermediate state between ignorance and wisdom. His parentage accounts for his condition, being the child of a wise and well-provided father, and of a mother both ignorant and poor.

"'Such is the daemoniacal nature, my dear Socrates; [c] nor do I wonder at your error concerning Love, for you thought, as I conjecture from what you say, that Love was not the lover but the beloved, and thence, well concluded that he must be supremely beautiful; for that which is the object of Love must indeed be fair, and delicate, and perfect, and most happy; but Love inherits, as I have declared, a totally opposite nature.' — 'Your words have persuasion in them, O stranger,' I said; 'be it as you say. But this Love, what advantages does he afford to men?' — [d] 'I will proceed to explain it to you, Socrates. Love being such and so produced as I have described, is, indeed, as you say, the love of things which are beautiful. But if any one should ask us, saying: O Socrates and Diotima, why is Love the love of beautiful things? Or, in plainer words, what does the lover of that which is beautiful, love in the object of his love, and seek from it?' — 'He seeks,' I said, interrupting her, 'the property and possession of it.' — 'But that,' she replied, 'might still be met with another question, What has he, that possesses that which is beautiful?' — 'Indeed, I cannot immediately reply.' — [e] 'But if, changing the beautiful for good, any one should enquire, — I ask, O Socrates, what is that which he who loves that which is good, loves in the object of his love?' — 'To be in his possession,' I replied. — 'And what has he, who has the possession of good?' — 'This question is of easier solution: he is happy.'* — [205a] 'Those who are happy, then, are happy through the possession; and it is useless to enquire what he desires, who desires to be happy; the question seems to have a complete reply. But do you think that this wish and this love are common to all men, and that all desire, that which is good should be for ever present to them?' — 'Certainly, common to all.' —

'Why do we not say then, Socrates, that every one loves? [b] if, indeed, all love perpetually the same thing? But we say that some love, and some do not.' — 'Indeed I wonder why it is so.' — 'Wonder not,' said Diotima, 'for we select a particular species of love, and apply to it distinctively the appellation of that which is universal.' —

'"Give me an example of such a select application.' — 'Poetry; which is a general name signifying every cause whereby anything proceeds from that which is not, into that which is; [c] so that the exercise of every inventive art is poetry, and all such artists poets.* Yet they are not called poets, but distinguished by other names; and one portion or species of poetry, that which has relation to music and rhythm, is divided from all others, and known by the name belonging to all. For this is alone properly called poetry, and those who exercise the art of this species of poetry, poets. [d] So, with respect to Love. Love is indeed universally all that earnest desire for the possession of happiness and that which is good; the greatest and the subtlest love, and which inhabits the heart of every human being; but those who seek this object through the acquirement of wealth, or the exercise of the gymnastic arts, or philosophy, are not said to love, nor are called lovers; one species alone is called Love, and those alone are said to be lovers, and to love, who seek the attainment of the universal desire through one species of Love, which is peculiarly distinguished by the name belonging to the whole. [e] It is asserted by some, that they love, who are seeking the lost half of their divided being. But I assert, that Love is neither the love of half or of the whole, unless, my friend, it meets with that which is good; since men willingly cut off their own hands and feet, if they think that they are the cause of evil to them. Nor do they cherish and embrace that which may belong to themselves, merely because it is their own; unless, indeed, any one should choose to say, that that which is good is attached to his own nature and is his own, whilst that which is evil is foreign and accidental; *[206a]* since men love nothing but that which is good. Does it not appear so to you?' — 'Assuredly.' — 'Can we then simply affirm that men love that which is good?' — 'Without doubt.' — 'What, then, must we not add, that, in addition to loving that which is good, they love that it should be present to themselves?' — 'Indeed that must be added.' — 'And not merely that it should be present, but that it should ever be present?' — 'This also must be added.'

'"Love, then, is collectively the desire in men that good should be for ever present to them.' — 'Most true.' — *[b]* 'Since this is the general definition of Love, can you explain in what mode of attaining its object, and in what species of actions, does Love peculiarly consist?' — 'If I knew what you ask, O Diotima, I should not have so much wondered at your wisdom, or have sought you out for the purpose of deriving improvement from your instructions.' — 'I will tell you then,' she replied: 'Love is the desire of generation in the beautiful, both with relation to the body and the soul.' — 'I must be a diviner to comprehend what you say, for, being such as I am, I confess that I do not understand it.' — *[c]* 'But I will explain it more clearly. The bodies and the souls of all human beings are alike pregnant with their future progeny, and when we arrive at a certain age, our nature impels us to bring forth and propagate. This nature is unable to produce in that which is deformed, but it can produce in that which is beautiful. The intercourse of the male and female in generation, a divine work, through pregnancy and production, is, as it were, something immortal in mortality. These things cannot take place in that which is incongruous; [d] for that which is deformed is incongruous, but that which is beautiful is congruous with what is immortal and divine. Beauty is, therefore, the Fate and the Juno Lucina* to generation. Wherefore, whenever that which is pregnant with the generative principle, approaches that which is beautiful, it becomes transported with delight, and is poured forth in overflowing pleasure, and propagates. But when it approaches that which is deformed, it is contracted and sad, and it is repelled and checked and does not produce, but retains unwillingly that with which it is pregnant. Wherefore, to one pregnant, and, as it were, already bursting with the load of his desire, [e] the impulse towards that which is beautiful is intense, on account of the great pain of retaining that which he has conceived. Love, then, O Socrates, is not as you imagine the love of the beautiful.' — 'What, then?' — 'Of generation and production in the beautiful.' — 'Why then of generation?' — 'Generation is something eternal and immortal in mortality. [207a] It necessarily, from what has been confessed, follows, that we must desire immortality together with what is good, since Love is the desire that good be for ever present to us. Of necessity Love must also be the desire of immortality.'

"Diotima taught me all this doctrine in the discourse we had together concerning Love; and in addition, she enquired, 'What do you think, Socrates, is the cause of this love and desire? Do you not perceive how all animals, both those of the earth and of the air, are affected when they

desire the propagation of their species, *[b]* affected even to
weakness and disease by the impulse of their love; first,
longing to be mixed with each other, and then seeking
nourishment for their offspring, so that the feeblest are
ready to contend with the strongest in obedience to this law,
and to die for the sake of their young, or to waste away with
hunger, and do or suffer anything so that they may not want
nourishment. It might be said that human beings do these
things through reason, *[c]* but can you explain why other
animals are thus affected through love?' — I confessed that
I did not know. — 'Do you imagine yourself,' said she, 'to
be skilful in the science of Love, if you are ignorant of these
things?' — 'As I said before, O Diotima, I come to you, well
knowing how much I am in need of a teacher. But explain
to me, I entreat you, the cause of these things, and of the
other things relating to Love.' — 'If,' said Diotima, 'you
believe that Love is of the same nature as we have mutually
agreed upon, wonder not that such are its effects. *[d]* For the
mortal nature seeks, so far as it is able, to become deathless
and eternal. But it can only accomplish this desire by generation, which for ever leaves another new in place of the
old. For, although each human being be severally said to
live, and be the same from youth to old age, yet, that which
is called the same, never contains within itself the same
things, but always is becoming new by the loss and change
of that which it possessed before; both the hair, and the
flesh, and the bones, and the entire body.

[e] "'And not only does this change take place in the
body, but also with respect to the soul. Manners, morals,
opinions, desires, pleasures, sorrows, fears; none of these
ever remain unchanged in the same persons; but some die
away, and others are produced. *[208a]* And, what is yet more

strange, that not only does some knowledge spring up, and another decay, and that we are never the same with respect to our knowledge, but that each several object of our thoughts suffers the same revolution. That which is called meditation, or the exercise of memory, is the science of the escape or departure of knowledge; for, forgetfulness is the going out of knowledge; and meditation, calling up a new memory in the place of that which has departed, preserves knowledge; so that, tho' for ever displaced and restored, it seems to be the same. In this manner every thing mortal is preserved: *[b]* not that it is constant and eternal, like that which is divine; but that in the place of what has grown old and is departed, it leaves another new like that which it was itself. By this contrivance, O Socrates, does what is mortal, the body and all other things, partake of immortality; that which is immortal, is immortal in another manner. Wonder not, then, if every thing by nature cherishes that which was produced from itself, for this earnest Love is a tendency towards eternity.'

"Having heard this discourse, I was astonished, and asked, 'Can these things be true, O wisest Diotima?' *[c]* And she, like an accomplished sophist, said, 'Know well, O Socrates, that if you only regard that love of glory which inspires men, you will wonder at your own unskilfulness in not having discovered all that I now declare. Observe with how vehement a desire they are affected to become illustrious and to prolong their glory into immortal time, to attain which object, *[d]* far more ardently than for the sake of their children, all men are ready to engage in any dangers, and expend their fortunes, and submit to any labours and incur any death. Do you believe that Alcestis would have died in the place of Admetus, or Achilles for the revenge of

Patroclus, or Codrus* for the kingdom of his posterity, if
they had not believed that the immortal memory of their
actions, which we now cherish, would have remained after
their death? Far otherwise; all such deeds are done for the
sake of ever-living virtue, and this immortal glory which
they have obtained; *[e]* and inasmuch as any one is of an
excellent nature, so much the more is he impelled to attain
this reward. For they love what is immortal.

    "'Those whose bodies alone are pregnant with this prin-
ciple of immortality are attracted by women, seeking
through the production of children what they imagine to be
happiness and immortality and an enduring remembrance;
[209a] but they whose souls are far more pregnant than
their bodies, conceive and produce that which is more suitable to the soul. What is suitable to the soul? Intelligence,
and every other power and excellence of the mind, of which
all poets, and all other artists who are creative and inventive,
are the authors. The greatest and most admirable wisdom is
that which regulates the government of families and states,
and which is called moderation and justice. *[b]* Whosoever,
therefore, from his youth feels his soul pregnant with the
conception of these excellencies, is divine; and when due
time arrives, desires to bring forth; and wandering about, he
seeks the beautiful in which he may propagate what he has
conceived; for there is no generation in that which is
deformed; he embraces those bodies which are beautiful
rather than those which are deformed, in obedience to the
principle within him which is ever seeking to perpetuate
itself. And if he meets, in conjunction with loveliness of
form, a beautiful, generous and gentle soul, he embraces
both at once, *[c]* and immediately undertakes to educate this
object of his love, and is inspired with an overflowing

persuasion to declare what is virtue, and what he ought to
be who would attain to its possession, and what are the
duties which it exacts. For, by the intercourse with, and as
it were, the very touch of that which is beautiful, he brings
forth and produces what he had formerly conceived; and
nourishes and educates that which is thus produced together with the object of his love, whose image, whether absent
or present, is never divided from his mind. So that those
who are thus united are linked by a nobler community and
a firmer love, as being the common parents of a lovelier and
more enduring progeny than the parents of other children.
[d] And every one who considers what posterity Homer and
Hesiod and the other great poets have left behind them, the
sources of their own immortal memory and renown, or
what children of his soul Lycurgus* has appointed to be the
guardians, not only of Lacedaemon, but of all Greece; or
what an illustrious progeny of laws Solon has produced, [e]
and how many admirable achievements, both among the
Greeks and Barbarians, men have left as the pledges of that
love which subsisted between them and the beautiful,
would choose rather to be the parent of such children than
those in an human shape. For divine honours have often
been rendered to them on account of such children, but on
account of those in human shape, never.

[210a] "Your own meditation, O Socrates, might perhaps have initiated you in all these things which I have
already taught you on the subject of Love. But those perfect and sublime ends, to which these are only the means, I
know not that you would have been competent to discover.
I will declare them, therefore, and will render them as intel-
ligible as possible: do you meanwhile strain all your attention to trace the obscure depth of the subject. He who

aspires to love rightly, ought from his earliest youth to seek
an intercourse with beautiful forms, and first to make a single form* the object of his love, and therein to generate intellectual excellencies. *[b]* He ought, then, to consider that
beauty in whatever form it resides is the brother of that
beauty which subsists in another form; and if he ought to
pursue that which is beautiful in form, it would be absurd to
imagine that beauty is not one and the same thing in all
forms, and would therefore remit much of his ardent preference towards one, through his perception of the multitude of claims upon his love. In addition, he would consider the beauty which is in souls more excellent than that
which is in form. So that one endowed with an admirable
soul, *[c]* even though the flower of his form were withered,
would suffice him as the object of his love and care, and the
companion with whom he might seek and produce such
conclusions as tend to the improvement of youth; so that it
might be led to observe the beauty and the conformity
which there is in the observation of its duties and the laws,
and to esteem little the mere beauty of the outward form.
The lover would then conduct his pupil to science, so that
he might look upon the loveliness of wisdom; and that contemplating thus the universal beauty, no longer would he,
like some servant in love, unworthily and meanly enslave
himself to the attractions of one form, nor one subject of
discipline or science, *[d]* but would turn towards the wide
ocean of intellectual beauty, and from the sight of the lovely and majestic forms which it contains, would abundantly
bring forth his conceptions in philosophy; until, strengthened and confirmed, he should at length steadily contemplate one science, which is the science of this universal
beauty.

[e] "'Attempt, I entreat you, to mark what I say with as keen an observation as you can. He who has been disciplined to this point in Love, by contemplating beautiful objects gradually, and in their order, now arriving at the end of all that concerns Love, on a sudden* beholds a beauty wonderful in its nature. This it is, O Socrates, for the sake of which all the former labours were endured. *[211a]* It is eternal, unproduced, indestructible; neither subject to encrease nor decay: not, like other things, partly beautiful and partly deformed; not at one time beautiful and at another time not; not beautiful in relation to one thing and deformed in relation to another; not here beautiful and there deformed; not beautiful in the estimation of one person and deformed in that of another; nor can this supreme beauty be figured to the imagination like a beautiful face, or beautiful hands, or any portion of the body, nor like any discourse, or any science. Nor does it subsist in any other thing that lives or is, either in earth, or in heaven, or in any other place; *[b]* but it is eternally uniform and consistent, and monoeidic* with itself. All other things are beautiful through a participation of it, with this condition, that although they are subject to production and decay, it never becomes more or less, or endures any change. When any one, ascending from a correct system of Love, begins to contemplate this supreme beauty, he already touches the consummation of his labour. *[c]* For such as discipline themselves upon this system, or are conducted by another, begin to ascend through these transitory objects which are beautiful, towards that which is beauty itself, proceeding as on steps from the love of one form to that of two, and from that of two, to that of all forms which are beautiful; and from beautiful forms to beautiful habits and institutions,

and from institutions to beautiful doctrines; until, from the meditation of many doctrines, they arrive at that which is nothing else than the doctrine of the supreme beauty itself, in the knowledge and contemplation of which at length they repose.

[d] "'Such a life as this, my dear Socrates,' exclaimed the stranger prophetess, 'spent in the contemplation of the beautiful, is the life for men to live; which if you chance ever to experience, you will esteem far beyond gold and rich garments, and even beyond those lovely persons whom you and many others now gaze on with astonishment, and are prepared neither to eat or drink so that you may behold and live for ever with, these objects of your love! *[e]* What, then, shall we imagine to be the aspect of the supreme beauty itself, simple, pure, uncontaminated with the intermixture of human flesh and colours, and all other idle and unreal shapes attendant on mortality; the divine, the original, the supreme, the self consistent, the monoeidic beautiful itself? *[212a]* What must be the life of him who dwells with and gazes on that which it becomes us all to seek? Think you not that to him alone is accorded the prerogative of bringing forth, not images and shadows of virtue, for he is in contact not with a shadow but with reality; with virtue itself, in the production and nourishment of which he becomes dear to the Gods, and if such a priviledge is conceded to any human being, himself immortal.'

[b] "Such, O Phaedrus, and my other friends, was what Diotima said. And being persuaded by her words, I have since occupied myself in attempting to persuade others, that it is not easy to find a better assistant than Love in seeking to communicate immortality to our human natures. Wherefore I exhort every one to honour Love; I hold him

in honour, and chiefly exercise myself in amatory matters, and exhort others to do so; and now and ever do I praise the power and excellence of Love, in the best manner that I can. *[c]* Let this discourse, if it pleases you, Phaedrus, be considered as an encomium of Love; or call it by what other name you will."

The whole assembly praised his discourse, and Aristophanes was on the point of making some remarks on the allusion made by Socrates to him in a part of his discourse, when suddenly they heard a loud knocking at the door of the vestibule, and a clamour as of revellers, attended by a flute-player. — *[d]* "Go, boys," said Agathon, "and see who is there: if they are any of our friends, call them in; if not, say that we have already done drinking." — A minute afterwards, they heard the voice of Alcibiades in the vestibule excessively drunk and roaring out: — "Where is Agathon? Lead me to Agathon!" — The flute-player, and some of his companions, then led him in, and placed him against the door-post, *[e]* crowned with a thick crown of ivy and violets, and having a quantity of fillets on his head. — "My friends," he cried out, "hail! I am excessively drunk already, but I'll drink with you, if you will. If not, we will go away after having crowned Agathon, for which purpose I came. I assure you that I could not come yesterday, but I am now here with these fillets round my temples, that from my own head I may crown his head who, with your leave, is the most beautiful and wisest of men. Are you laughing at me because I am drunk? *[213a]* Aye, I know what I say is true, whether you laugh or not. But tell me at once, whether I shall come in, or no. Will you drink with me?"

Agathon and the whole party desired him to come in, and recline among them; so he came in, led by his companions. He then unbound his fillets that he might crown Agathon, and though Socrates was just before his eyes, he did not see him, *[b]* but sat down by Agathon, between Socrates and him, for Socrates moved out of the way to make room for him. When he sat down, he embraced Agathon and crowned him; and Agathon desired the slaves to untie his sandals, that he might make a third, and recline on the same couch. "By all means," said Alcibiades, "but what third companion have we here?" And at the same time turning round and seeing Socrates, he leaped up and cried out — "O Hercules! what have we here? *[c]* You, Socrates, lying in ambush for me wherever I go! and meeting me just as you always do, when I least expected to see you! And, now, what are you come here for? Why have you chosen to recline exactly in this place, and not near Aristophanes, or any one else who is, or wishes to be ridiculous, but have contrived to lie down beside the most beautiful person of the whole party?" — "Agathon," said Socrates, "see if you cannot defend me. I declare my love for this man is a bad business: *[d]* from the moment that I first began to love him I have never been permitted to converse with, or so much as to look on any one who is beautiful. If I do, he is so jealous and suspicious that he does the most extravagant things, and hardly refrains from beating me. I entreat you to prevent him from doing anything of that kind at present. Procure a reconciliation: or, if he perseveres in attempting any violence, I entreat you to defend me, for I am seriously alarmed at the fury of his amatory impulse." — "Indeed," said Alcibiades, "I will not be reconciled to you; I shall find another opportunity to punish you for this. *[e]* But now," said he, addressing Agathon, "lend me some of those fillets, that I may crown the wonderful head of this fellow, lest I incur the blame, that having crowned you, I neglected to crown him who conquers all men with his discourses, not yesterday alone as you did, but ever."

Saying this he took the fillets, and having bound the head of Socrates, and again having reclined, said: "Come, my friends, you seem to be sober enough. You must not flinch, but drink, for that was your agreement with me before I came in. I choose as president, until you have drunk enough — myself. Come, Agathon, if you have got a great goblet, fetch it out. But no matter, that wine-cooler will do; bring it, boy!" *[214a]* And observing that it held more than eight cups, he first drank it off, and then ordered it to be filled for Socrates, and said: — "Observe, my friends, I cannot invent any scheme against Socrates, for he will drink as much as any one desires him, and not be in the least drunk." Socrates, after the boy had filled up, drank it off; and Eryximachus said: — *[b]* "Shall we then have no conversation or singing over our cups, but drink down stupidly, just as if we were thirsty?" And Alcibiades said: — "Ah, Eryximachus, I did not see you before; hail, you excellent son of a wise and excellent father!" — "Hail to you also," replied Eryximachus, "but what shall we do?" — "Whatever you command, for we ought to submit to your directions; a physician is worth an hundred common men. Command us as you please." — "Listen then," said Eryximachus; *[c]* "before you came in, each of us had agreed to deliver as eloquent a discourse as he could in praise of Love, beginning at the right hand; all the rest of us have fulfilled our engagement; you have not spoken, and yet have drunk with us: you ought to bear your part in the discussion; and having done so, command what you please to Socrates, who shall have the priviledge of doing so to his right-hand neighbour, and so on to the others." — "Indeed, there appears some justice in your proposal, Eryximachus, though it is rather unfair to induce a drunken man to set his discourse in competition with that of those who are sober. *[d]* And, besides, did Socrates really persuade you that what he just said about me was true, or do you not know that matters are in fact exactly the reverse of his representation? For I seriously believe that, should I praise in his presence, be he God or man, any other beside himself, he would not keep his hands off me." — "Good words I entreat you," said Socrates — "I charge you by Neptune," cried Alcibiades, "to keep quiet, I assure you that I will praise no one beside yourself in your presence."

"Do so, then," said Eryximachus; "praise Socrates if you please." — *[e]* "What!" said Alcibiades, "shall I attack him, and punish him before you all?" — "What have you got into your head now," said Socrates; "are you going to expose me to ridicule, and to misrepresent me? Or what are you going to do?" — "I will only speak the truth; will you permit me on this condition?" — "I not only permit, but exhort you to say all the truth you know," replied Socrates. "I obey you willingly," said Alcibiades; "and if I advance anything untrue, do you, if you please, interrupt me, and convict me of misrepresentation, for I would never willingly speak falsely. *[215a]* And bear with me if I do not relate things in their order, but just as I remember them, for it is not easy for a man in my present condition to enumerate systematically all your singularities.

"I will begin the praise of Socrates by comparing him to a certain statue.* Perhaps he will think that this statue* is introduced for the sake of ridicule, but I assure you that it is necessary for the illustration of truth. *[b]* I assert, then, that

Socrates is exactly like those Silenuses* that sit in the sculp-
tors' shops, and which are carved holding flutes or pipes,
but which, when divided in two, are found to contain with-
inside the images of the Gods.* I assert that Socrates is like
the satyr Marsyas.* That your form and appearance are like
these Satyrs, I think that even you will not venture to deny;
and how like you are to them in all other things, now hear.
Are you not scornful and petulant? If you deny this, I will
bring witnesses. Are you not a piper, and far more wonderful a one than he? [c] For Marsyas, and whoever now pipes
the music that he taught — for that music which is of heav-
en and described as being taught by Marsyas enchants men
through the power of the mouth — for if any musician, be
he skilful or not,* awakens this music, it alone enables him
to retain the minds of men, and from the divinity of its
nature makes evident those who are in want of the Gods
and initiation. You differ only from Marsyas in this circumstance, that you effect without instruments, by mere words,
all that he can do. [d] For when we hear Pericles,* or any
other accomplished orator, deliver a discourse, no one, as it
were, cares anything about it. But when any one hears you,
or even your words related by another, though ever so rude
and unskilful a speaker, be that person a woman, man or
child, we are struck and retained, as it were, by the discourse clinging to our mind.

"If I was not afraid that I am a great deal too drunk, I
would confirm to you by an oath the strange effects which
I assure you I have suffered from his words, and suffer still;
[e] for when I hear him speak, my heart leaps up far more
than the hearts of those who celebrate the Corybantic mysteries;* my tears are poured out as he talks, a thing I have
seen happen to many others beside myself. I have heard

Pericles and other excellent orators, and have been pleased with their discourses, but I suffered nothing of this kind; nor was my soul ever on those occasions disturbed and filled with self-reproach, as if it were slavishly laid prostrate. *[216a]* But this Marsyas here has often affected me in the way I describe, until the life which I lead seemed hardly worth living. Do not deny it, Socrates; for I well know that if even now I chose to listen to you, I could not resist, but should again suffer the same effects. For, my friends, he forces me to confess that while I myself am still in want of many things, I neglect my own necessities, and attend to those of the Athenians. I stop my ears, therefore, as from the Syrens,* and flee away as fast as possible, that I may not sit down beside him and grow old in listening to his talk. *[b]* For this man has reduced me to feel the sentiment of shame, which I imagine no one would readily believe was in me; he alone inspires me with remorse and awe. For I feel in his presence my incapacity of refuting what he says, or of refusing to do that which he directs; but when I depart from him, the glory which the multitude confers overwhelms me. I escape, therefore, and hide myself from him, and when I see him I am overwhelmed with humiliation, because I have neglected to do what I have confessed to him ought to be done; *[c]* and often and often have I wished that he were no longer to be seen among men. But if that were to happen, I well know that I should suffer far greater pain; so that where I can turn, or what I can do with this man, I know not. All this have I and many others suffered from the pipings of this satyr.

"And observe how like he is to what I said, and what a wonderful power he possesses. *[d]* Know that there is not one of you who is aware of the real nature of Socrates; but since I have begun, I will make him plain to you. You observe how passionately Socrates affects the intimacy of those who are beautiful, and how ignorant he professes himself to be; appearances in themselves excessively Silenic. This, my friends, is the external form with which, like one of those sculptured Silenuses, he has clothed himself; for if you open him, you will find within admirable temperance and wisdom. For he cares not for mere beauty, *[e]* but despises more than any one can imagine all external possessions, whether it be beauty or wealth, or glory, or any other thing for which the multitude felicitates the possessor. He esteems these things and us who honour them, as nothing, and lives among men, making all the objects of their admiration the playthings of his irony. But I know not if any one of you have ever seen the divine images which are within, when he has been opened and is serious. *[217a]* I have seen them, and they are so supremely beautiful, so golden, so divine, and wonderful, that every thing which Socrates commands surely ought to be obeyed, even like the voice of a God.*

"On our first intimacy I imagined that Socrates was in love with me on account of my beauty, and was determined to seize so favourable an opportunity, by conceding to him all that he required, of learning from him all that he knew: for I imagined that my beauty was something irresistable and extraordinary. *[b]* As soon as I perceived this I sent away the servant, who was accustomed to be present at our meetings, and remained with him alone: for I will tell you the whole truth, therefore now attend; and do you, Socrates, if I say anything that is false, interrupt and refute me. Well,

he and I were now alone together and I thought that he
would then say all that a lover is accustomed to say in solitude to his beloved, and was rejoiced. But nothing of this
kind passed, and after spending the day with me, and talking just as usual, he went away. *[c]* After this I invited him to
exercise with me in gymnastic exercises, hoping that something might arise out of this; and we were very often stript
and wrestled together with no other person present. What
is the use of more words? Everything failed; and since I
could not succeed thus I resolved having once taken it into
hand to assail him with more powerful temptations; and
now I have once begun I will tell all.

"I invited him to supper, actually laying plots for him as
a lover would for his beloved. *[d]* At first he would not
accept my invitation, but at last being persuaded he came
and went away immediately after supper. I was ashamed that
time of what I had undertaken and let him go. But laying
my plan a second time, I protracted the conversation after
supper far into the night, and when he motioned to depart,
I prevailed on him to remain, alledging the lateness of the
hour. He composed himself to sleep on the couch next to
mine on which he had supped: and no one else slept in the
house beside ourselves. *[e]* So much as this I could relate
without difficulty to any one; but I cannot proceed further
without reminding you of the proverb that, wine tells truth,
whether with or without youth. I cannot pass over, though
I have undertaken to praise Socrates, so proud and scornful
a deed. Besides I am like one bitten by a viper, who they say
will not tell his misfortune to any, but those who are bitten
in the same manner, *[218a]* since they alone knowing what
it is, will pardon him for whatever he dares to do or say
under the mitigation of his pain. I then, bitten by something

more keen and vehement than the keenest of all things by
which any one ever was bitten, wounded in my very heart
and soul or whatever else you choose to call it, by the words
of philosophy which pierce more sharply than a viper's
tooth, when they seize on a fresh and not ungenerous spirit, and instigate it to say or do anything, *[b]* seeing
Phaedrus, and Agathon, and Eryximachus, and Pausanias,
and Aristodemus, and Aristophanes, and Socrates himself,
and the rest of our companions; for ye are all participators
with me in the sacred madness and bacchic enthusiasm of
philosophy, am willing that you should hear all. Pardon, I
entreat you, what then was done and now is said. Let the
servants, or if any other prophane and unrefined person is
present, close their ears with impenetrable gates.

[c] "Well, my friends, as soon as the attendants had
withdrawn and the lamp was extinguished I determined to
hesitate no longer but plainly to speak my mind. Touching
him, therefore, I said: — 'Socrates are you asleep?' — 'Not
I,' said he. — 'Do you know what I have been thinking of?'
— 'Well, what is it?' — 'Why,' said I, 'I esteem you to be
the only lover worthy of me, but I imagine that although
you feel such tenderness for me as lovers feel, you are
ashamed to confess your sentiments. Being such as I am, I
should consider myself indeed unwise if I were not prepared to make every return you can desire to your preference, as I would willingly gratify you, not only in this, but
in every thing else that my fortune and connexion can command; *[d]* for it has been my earliest ambition to become as
virtuous and accomplished as possible, nor can I conceive
any companion or guide more excellent than you to conduct me in the path of its attainment; and not conceding all
that such a man as you could desire, I should more dread

the reproaches of the wise, than conceding it, the idle clamours of the multitude.' — Hearing this, Socrates said ironically and just in his way — [e] 'My dear Alcibiades, if what you say of me be true, and if there be any power in me through which you may become better, you must see methinks some very uncommon beauty in me, very different from that loveliness which is so conspicuous in yourself. If you seek my intercourse for the sake of this, and would exchange your beauty against mine, you design no doubt to gain considerably by me: you would possess that which is truly beautiful instead of the opinion and appearance of beauty, gold instead of brass.* [219a] But my dear friend, observe lest you be deceived in me, and I be indeed nothing. The vision of the understanding then grows keen when the radiance of youth first wanes in the eyes, and yours are yet far from this.' — Hearing this I said: 'My sentiments are such as I have expressed. I have said nothing that I do not mean. Do you only determine what is best for yourself and me.' — 'This is well,' he replied, [b] 'for the future we will consider what is best to be done; both concerning what you propose, and concerning all other things.' — After this conversation I believed and hoped that my words had wounded him as with a weapon, so rising from my couch and permitting him to say no more, and casting this garment around us both (for it was winter) [c] I lay the whole night with my arms around this truly divine and wonderful being, upon that very old cloak that he has got on now. I know, Socrates, that you cannot deny what I alledge. He despised and contemptuously neglected that beauty which I had thus exposed to his rejection, O Judges, for you shall be judges of the insolence of Socrates: know then, by all the Gods and Goddesses, [d] I swear that I awoke and arose from as

unimpassioned an embrace as if I had slept with my father
or my elder brother. And after this what think you was the
contest of my mind, feeling that I had been thus dishon-
oured, and yet loving the courage, and temperance and wisdom with which I found this man endowed, so excellently
as I had not believed could have fallen to the lot of any
human being. So that I could neither persevere in my
indignation against, or deprive myself of an intercourse
with him, [e] or discover any attraction with which I might
entice him to my society. For I knew that he was less vulnerable by money than Ajax by iron,* and that resource
alone with which I had endeavoured to captivate him, had
already failed me. I became the prey of doubt and trouble,
and enslaved to this man far more than any other was ever
enslaved, I wandered about disconsolately. Such as I have
declared was the event of what I attempted.

"Some time after this, we were fellow-soldiers, and had
our mess together in the camp before Potidaea. Socrates
there overcame not only me, but everyone beside, in
endurance of toils: when, as often happens in a campaign,
[220a] we were reduced to few provisions, there were none
who could sustain hunger like Socrates; and when he had
plenty, he alone seemed to enjoy our military fare. He
never drank much willingly, but when he was compelled, he
conquered all even in that to which he was least accustomed; and what is most astonishing, no person ever saw
Socrates drunk either then or at any other time. In the
depth of winter (and the winters there are excessively rigid),
[b] he sustained calmly incredible hardships: and amongst
other things, whilst the frost was intolerably severe, and no
one went out of their tents, or if they went out, wrapt themselves up carefully, and put fleeces under their feet, and

bound their legs with hairy skins, Socrates went out only with the same cloak on that he usually wore, and walked barefoot upon the ice; more easily, indeed, than those who had sandalled themselves so delicately: *[c]* so that the soldiers thought that he did it to mock their want of fortitude. It would indeed be worth while to commemorate all that this brave man did and endured in that expedition. In one instance he was seen early in the morning, standing in one place wrapt in meditation; and as he seemed not to be able to unravel the subject of his thoughts, he still continued to stand as enquiring and discussing within himself, and when noon came, the soldiers observed him, and said to one another — 'Socrates has been standing there thinking, ever since the morning.' *[d]* At last some Ionians came to the spot, and having supped, as it was summer, bringing their blankets, they lay down to sleep in the cool; they observed that Socrates continued to stand there the whole night until morning, and that, when the sun rose, he saluted it with a prayer and departed.

"I ought not to omit what Socrates is in battle. For in that battle after which the generals decreed to me the prize of courage, *[e]* Socrates alone of all men was the saviour of my life, standing by me when I had fallen and was wounded, and preserving both myself and my arms from the hands of the enemy. On that occasion I entreated the generals to decree the prize, as it was most due, to him. And this, O Socrates, you cannot deny, that the generals, wishing to conciliate a person of my rank, desired to give me the prize; you were far more earnestly desirous than the generals that this glory should be attributed not to yourself, but me.

[221a] "But to see Socrates when our army was defeated and scattered in flight at Delium, was a spectacle worthy to

behold. On that occasion I was among the cavalry, and he
on foot, heavily armed. After the total rout of our troops,
he and Laches* retreated together; I came up by chance,
and seeing them, bade them be of good cheer, for that I
would not leave them. As I was on horseback, and therefore
less occupied by a regard of my own situation, I could better observe than at Potidaea the beautiful spectacle exhibited by Socrates on this emergence. *[b]* How superior was he
to Laches in presence of mind and courage! Your representation of him on the stage, O Aristophanes, was not wholly
unlike his real self on this occasion, for 'he walked and darted his regards around with a majestic composure,'* looking
tranquilly both on his friends and enemies; so that it was
evident to every one, even from afar, that whoever should
venture to attack him would encounter a desperate resist-
ance. He and his companion thus departed in safety; *[c]* for
those who are scattered in flight are pursued and killed,
whilst men hesitate to touch those who exhibit such a coun-
tenance as that of Socrates even in defeat.

"Many other and most wonderful qualities might well
be praised in Socrates; but such as these might singly be
attributed to others. But that which is unparalleled in
Socrates, is, that he is unlike, and above comparison, with
all other men, whether those who have lived in ancient
times, or those who exist now. For it may be conjectured,
that Brasidas* and many others are such as was Achilles.
Pericles deserves comparison with Nestor* and Antenor;*
[d] and other excellent persons of various times may, with
probability, be drawn into comparison with each other. But
to such a singular man as this, both himself and his discourses are so uncommon, no one, should he seek, would
find a parallel among the present or the past generations of

mankind; unless they should say that he resembled those with whom I lately compared him, for, assuredly, he and his discourses are like nothing but the Silenuses and the Satyrs. At first I forgot to make you observe how like his discourses are to those Satyrs when they are opened, *[e]* for, if any one will listen to the talk of Socrates, it will appear to him at first extremely ridiculous; the phrases and expressions which he employs, fold around his exterior the skin, as it were, of a rude and wanton Satyr. He is always talking about great market-asses, and brass-founders, and leather-cutters, and skin-dressers; and this is his perpetual custom, *[222a]* so that any dull and unobservant person might easily laugh at his discourse. But if any one should see it opened, as it were, and get within the sense of his words, he would then find that they alone of all that enters into the mind of man to utter, had a profound and persuasive meaning, and that they were most divine; and that they presented to the mind innumerable images of every excellence, and that they tended towards objects of the highest moment, or rather towards all, that he who seeks the possession of what is supremely beautiful and good, need regard as essential to the accomplishment of his ambition.

"These are the things, my friends, for which I praise Socrates, as well as those which I complain of in him, for I have mixed up in my discourse the peculiar scorn with which he treated me. *[b]* Not that I have been the only object of his contempt, but Charmides,* the son of Glauco, and Euthydemus,* the son of Diodes, are deceived in the same manner, imagining that he was their lover, whilst in fact they vainly pursued him as the object of theirs. As to you, Agathon, take my advice; do not let him cheat you. Be admonished by my sufferings to take care, and not according to the proverb, like a fool grow wise by your own experience."

[c] Alcibiades having said this, the whole party burst into laughter at the frankness with which he seemed to confess that he was still in love with Socrates; and Socrates said, "You seem to be sober enough, Alcibiades, else you would not have made such a circuit of words, only to hide the main design for which you made this long speech, and which, as it were carelessly, you just throw in at the last; [d] now, as if you had not said all this for the mere purpose of dividing me and Agathon? You think that I ought to love you and no one else, and that Agathon ought to be loved by you and no one else. I have found you out; it is evident enough for what design you invented all this Satyrical and Silenic drama.* But, my dear Agathon, do not let his device succeed. I entreat you to permit no one to throw discord between us." — [e] "No doubt," said Agathon, "he sate down between us only that he might divide us; but this shall not assist his scheme, for I will come and recline near you." — "Do so," said Socrates, "come, there is room for you close under me." — "Oh, Jupiter!" exclaimed Alcibiades, "what I endure from that man! He thinks to subdue me every way; but, at least, I pray you, let Agathon recline between us." — "Impossible," said Socrates, "you have just praised me; I ought to praise him sitting at my right hand. If Agathon reclines under you, will he not praise me before I praise him? [223a] Now, my dear friend, allow the young man to receive what praise I can give him. I have a great desire to pronounce his encomium." — "Quick, quick, Alcibiades," said Agathon, "I cannot stay here, I must change my place, or Socrates will not praise me." — "This is just like him," said Alcibiades, "when Socrates is present

it is impossible to catch hold of any of those who are beautiful. I entreat you to observe how easily he found out a plausible pretext for this beautiful Agathon to come and lie down by him." — [b] Agathon then arose to take his place near Socrates.

He had no sooner reclined than there came in a number of revellers — for some one who had gone out had left the door open — and took their places on the vacant couches, and everything became full of confusion; and no order being observed, every one was obliged to drink a great quantity of wine. Eryximachus, and Phaedrus, and some others, said Aristodemus, went home to bed; that, for his part, he went to sleep on his couch, [c] and slept long and soundly — the nights were then long — until the cock crew in the morning. When he awoke he found that some were still fast asleep, and others had gone home, and that Aristophanes, Agathon, and Socrates had alone stood it out, and were still drinking out of a great goblet which they passed round and round. Socrates was disputing between them. [d] The beginning of their discussion Aristodemus said that he did not recollect, because he was asleep; but it was terminated by Socrates forcing them to confess, that the same person is able to compose both tragedy and comedy, and that the foundations of the tragic and comic arts were essentially the same. They, rather convicted than convinced, went to sleep. Aristophanes first fell asleep, and then, it being broad daylight, Agathon. Socrates, having put them to sleep, went away, Aristodemus following him; and coming to the Lyceum he washed himself, as he would have done anywhere else, and after having spent the day there in his accustomed manner, went home in the evening.

Notes

These notes comment on (1) unfamiliar historical or linguistic aspects of Plato's text, and (2) a few especially important idiosyncrasies or plain errors in Shelley's translation of the Greek text. I have let these occasional translation errors stand in the text, but I provide more accurate versions in the notes. In three places (191d, 191e, and 193a) where Shelley did not translate the Greek and simply put the transliterated Greek word into his text, I have substituted a translation. I have not modernized or systematized Shelley's spelling or punctuation.

Though Shelley's letters and the comments of the friends with whom he shared the manuscript make it clear that he worked carefully on the translation, he never prepared it for publication, and so it contains some minor errors in its English that he no doubt would have corrected himself. Since this edition is a text for the general reader rather than the scholar, I have not recorded such minor corrections. No autograph manuscript now exists, and we know the text only through a transcription made by Mary Shelley. Those interested in the curious history of the text's production, suppression, and bowdlerization, as well as in a critical edition of the text, should consult James A. Notopoulos, *The Platonism of Shelley*, Duke University Press, 1949. I have used Notopoulos' report of the transcription, though I have been somewhat more conservative than Notopoulos about emending this text.

The reader's appreciation of the *Symposium* will be enriched by knowledge of the cultural crises of the time, particularly concerning Alcibiades, the most charismatic and controversial Athenian of his age. I give a brief sketch of the political and religious background in the note to 172c, but the interested reader might enjoy Plutarch's much fuller account in his "Life of Alcibiades."

The notes are keyed to the bracketed page and section references in the text. For example, 181b is a reference to bracketed page number 181, section b. The bracketed page and section references, known as "Stephanus numbers," derive from a sixteenth-century edition of the Greek text by Henri Estienne, and provide a standard system of reference to Plato's works.

The Banquet: "Banquet" is Shelley's translation of the Greek *symposion*, literally a "drinking-together."

THE PERSONS OF THE DIALOGUE:

APOLLODORUS: Plato (*Phaedo*) and Xenophon (*Apology of Socrates to the Jury*) both portray Apollodorus as an unusually emotional and vehement admirer of Socrates and make a point of his softness or effeminacy. He is in his late twenties when he reports to Glauco, apparently around the time of Socrates' indictment, what he has been told about the party at Agathon's, which took place seventeen years earlier, in 416 BC (see 172c note).

A FRIEND OF APOLLODORUS: Like Glauco, this unnamed friend is interested in hearing from Apollodorus what

Agathon's party revealed about the relationship between Socrates and Alcibiades.

GLAUCO: Glauco is interested in hearing from Apollodorus what Agathon's party revealed about the relationship between Socrates and Alcibiades. He is so excited to learn more that he fails to realize how long ago the party must have taken place (see 172c note). He is about the same age as Apollodorus. This Glauco, whose name is introduced abruptly as if we are expected to know who he is, is very likely Plato's brother, who is Socrates' main interlocutor in Plato's *Republic*, where he is portrayed as a brilliant young man with great political ambitions and strong erotic desires. His name is now usually spelled "Glaucon."

ARISTODEMUS: At the time of Agathon's party, one of Socrates' most vehement admirers, whom Socrates brings along to the party and who later tells the story to Apollodorus.

SOCRATES: At the time of Agathon's party, Socrates is in his early fifties. He was executed seventeen years later, in 399 BC, on a charge of introducing strange divinities and corrupting the youth. His relationship to Alcibiades may have been an important part of the background to the charge (see 172c note).

AGATHON: An innovative and successful playwright, Agathon is usually considered the fourth greatest of the ancient tragedians, behind only Aeschylus, Sophocles, and Euripides. He apparently was notorious for his flamboyant cultivation of a sexually ambiguous personal style. He had an erotic relationship with his older lover Pausanias that lasted for some thirty years, until his death around 399 BC.

Pederastic relationships between teenage boys and adult men were not shocking in classical Greece, but this relationship was quite atypical, since younger males were normally expected to lose their erotic attractiveness to older males when they reached physical maturity in their late teens or early twenties. He was in his early thirties when he won first prize with his first entry in the tragic competitions, and this victory is the occasion for the party reported in the *Symposium*. He left Athens around 406 BC to live in Macedon at the court of his patron, King Archelaus.

PHAEDRUS: Implicated with Alcibiades in the profanation of the Eleusinian Mysteries a year after Agathon's party (see 172c note), Phaedrus is presented by Plato, here and in the *Phaedrus*, as especially interested in two topics, rhetoric and love. In both dialogues, he seems especially interested to defend the honorableness of the younger party in pederastic relationships. He is in his early thirties at Agathon's party, and seems to have been an especially close friend of Eryximachus (see 176d and 177a).

PAUSANIAS: Portrayed in Plato's *Protagoras* as Agathon's lover when Agathon was still only a teenager, Pausanias maintained their relationship throughout Agathon's adulthood (see **AGATHON** above). He appears to have emigrated to Macedon with Agathon around 406 BC.

ERYXIMACHUS: Implicated with Alcibiades in the profanation of the Eleusinian Mysteries a year after Agathon's party (see 172c note), Eryximachus is presented as a rather pompous devotee of the medical profession. He is in his early thirties at Agathon's party. He seems to have been an especially close friend of Phaedrus (see 176d and 177a).

ARISTOPHANES: The greatest comic dramatist of the ancient world, Aristophanes is probably around forty at Agathon's party. He is the only speaker at the party who is not involved in a special relationship of some sort with at least one of the other speakers. Seven years before the party, in 423 BC, he had produced *Clouds*, a sometimes biting lampoon of Socrates and the young men attracted to him.

ALCIBIADES: In his early thirties at Agathon's party, Alcibiades was then at the height of his political influence. He was famously charismatic and reckless, and Socrates' association with him seems to have contributed to Socrates' later indictment, conviction, and execution. At the height of his political career, he was implicated in the profanation of the Eleusinian Mysteries and forced into exile (see 172c note).

172a returning home from Phalerum: This phrase should say, "coming up to town from my home at Phalerum." Shelley mistakenly made the place Apollodorus was coming *from* when Glauco met him into the place he was going *to*.

172c Agathon has been absent from the city many years . . . . But since I began to converse with Socrates, . . . three years are scarcely past: By having Glauco be so excited that he doesn't think about how long ago Agathon's party with Socrates and Alcibiades must have been, Plato is able to suggest to the reader two questions in this passage: (1) When did the original party at Agathon's with Socrates and Alcibiades take place? (2) When did this old party again become important enough that two people, Glauco and an unnamed companion, asked Apollodorus about it in a couple of days? On (1): Apollodorus tells Glauco the party occurred when the two of them "were yet children . . . when Agathon first gained the prize of tragedy" (173a), that is, in 416 BC. This was a year before Alcibiades, Eryximachus, and Phaedrus were implicated in a political and religious scandal, the profanation of the Eleusinian Mysteries. The scandal derailed Alcibiades' political career at the height of his influence. The Eleusinian Mysteries, the most important religious event in Athens, centered on the initiation of participants, where they learned cult doctrine and celebrated a ritual culminating in the display of sacred objects. Neither the doctrines nor the objects could be revealed to the uninitiated. There are allusions to both aspects of the Mysteries in the *Symposium*; see especially Diotima's speech at 210a and 210e. On (2): Agathon left Athens around 407–406 BC. Apollodorus indicates Agathon has been gone quite a bit longer than the nearly three years Apollodorus has spent hanging on Socrates' every word and deed. (Shelley's "three years are scarcely past" means "not quite three years," not "barely more than three years.") So Apollodorus must be speaking at a time a few years later than 404–403 BC. What event in this time frame would explain why Apollodorus is asked twice in a couple of days to recount the meeting of Socrates and Alcibiades at Agathon's? The only strong candidate is the indictment of Socrates in 399 BC on the charge of introducing strange divinities and corrupting the youth, since his notorious relationship to Alcibiades was part of what lay behind the indictment (as Xenophon's *Memorabilia* makes clear). If these inferences can be trusted, Plato has given the dialogue a complicating political backdrop to go with the explicit focus on erotic love.

173b   by Jupiter: Shelley translated Greek names for gods and other mythical figures into their Latin equivalents:

> Jupiter = Zeus (the king of the gods)
>
> Bacchus = Dionysus (the god of wine, theater, and religious ecstasy)
>
> Venus = Aphrodite (the goddess of beauty and erotic love)
>
> Aesculapius = Asclepius (the divinized founder of medicine)
>
> Vulcan = Hephaestus (the god of metalworking; husband of Aphrodite; ugly and limping)
>
> Mars = Ares (the god of war; harsh and manly, but tamed by Aphrodite)
>
> Minerva = Athena (the goddess of intelligent crafts, such as weaving)

173d   the surname of "The Madman": The text from which Shelley translated was defective here, printing an inferior variant in the Greek manuscripts. His text read *manikos* = "mad, raving," while the superior reading is *malakos* = "soft, effeminate." A translation of the superior reading would say, "the surname of 'The Softy.'" Apollodorus' companion is saying, "I don't see why people call you a softy when you're always so hard on everyone but Socrates." The question of how male erotic relationships can live up to cultural ideals of hard, tough masculinity without sacrificing the soft and tender experiences of love is a major leitmotif of the *Symposium*. For other passages that explore this anxiety about softness, with words using the same root *mal-*, see for example 174c ("faint-hearted"), 179d ("cowardly"), 195d–e ("soft"); compare 203c–d.

174b 'To the feasts of the good': There is a pun on Agathon's name: *agathon* = "good."

175a recline there near Eryximachus: Agathon tells Aristodemus to recline on a couch with Eryximachus. — The reader will not understand some of the dialogue without understanding the seating arrangements at a Greek party. Agathon's room is furnished with about five wide, low couches, arranged in a circle. Guests recline on their backs diagonally on these couches, usually two to a couch, one on the top half, one on the bottom. They turn their upper body to the left and rest on their left elbow, facing the middle of the circle. Each has a small food table inside the circle, accessible to his right hand. The couch counter-clockwise from another couch is said to be "below" it. The speaking duties and the wine bowl are passed around counter-clockwise. Phaedrus reclines on the top half of the first couch, and so is the first speaker to give his encomium of Love (177d). Aristodemus did not remember the next few speakers, apparently including Phaedrus' couch-partner and a pair sharing a second couch (180c). Then Pausanias and Aristophanes share the third couch, while the fourth couch, which is "below" Aristophanes (185c, where Shelley's "close beside him" is more literally "beneath him"), is shared by Eryximachus and Aristodemus. Finally, the last couch has been arranged by Agathon to hold himself and Socrates (175c). When Alcibiades enters, he plops down on this last couch, with Agathon to his left, "above" him, and Socrates to his right, "below" him (213b). Alcibiades instigates a new round of speeches, each of which should be dedicated to praising the person to the speaker's right (214d, 222e). Agathon, wanting to receive Socrates' praises, is moving to squeeze onto the front of the couch, to Socrates' right (223b), when a crowd of revelers breaks in.

175c   At last he came in, much about the middle of supper, not having delayed so long as was his custom: Shelley inadvertently misplaced the negation in this sentence and so reversed its sense. It should say, "In a little while, he came in, much about the middle of supper, having finished his customary activity." The point is that Socrates did *not* let the dinner affect his usual habit of thinking things over when they occurred to him. This is an example of Socrates' general ability to remain himself and be unaffected, whether by wine (see 176c), love (see 219c–d), extremes of weather (see 220c), or fear in battle (see 220e–221a).

175e   taking Bacchus for our judge: Agathon has just won first prize in the dramatic competition, which had Bacchus as its patron deity; so on one level he is suggesting that he and Socrates will compete in their speeches like playwrights in the theater. But he is also suggesting that they will carry on their dispute when they have been drinking heavily, since Bacchus is the god of wine. Alcibiades will later invade the party wearing violets and ivy, two emblems of Bacchus, and award prizes to Agathon and Socrates, so Agathon's prediction about Bacchus coming in judgment is made literally true.

176c   invincible drinkers: Appropriately enough, Aristophanes and Agathon, whose lives are devoted to the theater and so to Bacchus, are also the biggest drinkers in the crowd.

178e   a state or army could be composed of lovers: Plato appears to put a prophecy in Phaedrus' mouth, alluding to a successful elite military unit organized of lovers and their beloveds, the so-called "Sacred Band" of Thebes. Since this unit was not organized before 378 BC, it is likely the dialogue was written sometime in the mid-370s.

179d   and thus to secure to himself a perpetual intercourse with her in the regions to which she had preceded him: This clause is an addition of Shelley's. Nothing in the Greek corresponds to it.

180a   not to die for him merely, but to disdain and reject that life which he had ceased to share: Phaedrus is saying Achilles died, not in order to save Patroclus (*hyperapothanein*), but even after Patroclus was beyond help (*epapothanein*). The contrast explains part of Phaedrus' ranking of Achilles over Alcestis: Alcestis died *on behalf of* her husband Admetus, whereas Achilles died *because of* or *in addition to* his lover Patroclus.

180d–e the eldest . . . we call the Uranian . . . the younger . . . we call the Pandemian: "Uranian" also means "heavenly," while "Pandemian" means "common" or "popular," which Pausanias takes to mean "vulgar." Aphrodite was in fact worshipped under these two different epithets.

182c   Harmodius and Aristogiton: Athenian national heroes who lived about a century before the *Symposium* takes place, this erotic couple were reputed to have provoked a democratic revolution by assassinating the tyrant then in power.

183c   masters: Shelley's translation of *paidagôgoi*. A *paidagôgos* is literally a "leader of children," and was generally a slave whose job was to chaperone a teenage boy. Such pedagogues were notoriously irresponsible and ineffective.

185c   to denote the changes of the discourse: This should say, "to speak in balanced phrases." Apparently Shelley did not understand the phrase *isa legein* = "to speak in balanced phrases." Apollodorus (or was it Aristodemus, being reported by Apollodorus?) is referring to the sound of *Pausaniou pausamenou* = "Pausanias having ceased."

187d   an extremely skilful artist: "artist" = *dêmiourgos*; see also 188d: "author" = *dêmiourgos*. More precisely, *dêmiourgos* = "craftsman." In the early nineteenth century, "artist" could still refer to a practitioner of a learned art, such as medicine or astronomy; yet throughout Eryximachus' speech, Shelley somewhat obscured Eryximachus' emphasis on the technical or craft nature of medicine, considered as the exemplar of erotic knowledge, and introduced a vocabulary that more easily includes poetry. See also 194a note and 205c note.

187e   Polymnia: Polymnia, like Urania, is one of the Muses. Her name means roughly "of many harmonies," and Eryximachus is implying that her multiplicity in the realm of music fits the sensuality and promiscuousness earlier attributed to Pandemian love.

190b   Ephialtes and Otus: In Homer, giants who plotted against the Olympian gods and were destroyed by Zeus.

191c   but from those of the same sex, no such consequence ensues: This is the first of three passages in Aristophanes' speech where Shelley toned down references to the physical expression of eros between males. He omitted the next sentence in 191c: "If a male entwines with a male, at least he would be satisfied by the intercourse and be done with it, and turn to his work and pay attention to the rest of his life." In 192a, Shelley wrote, "[Young men who are a section of the original double male] are delighted with the intercourse and familiarity of men." Aristophanes actually says, "[Such young men] love men, and enjoy lying and entwining with them." In 192b, Shelley wrote, "[Such a man becomes] an affectionate lover and a faithful friend." Aristophanes actually says, "It is such men who take up an erotic interest in boys [*paiderastês*], or who become attached to their lovers [*philerastês*]." Shelley avoids translating *paiderastês* = "boy-lover" or simply "pederast." See also 210a with note, for a similar softening in Diotima's speech.

191d   flatfish: Shelley's text reads *psetta*, which transliterates the Greek word for "flatfish."

191e   those who become adulteresses with female partners: Shelley's text reads, "the *Hetairistriae*," which transliterates the unusual Greek word *hetairistriai* = "adulteresses (with female partners)." Aristophanes distinguishes between women who come from an original male-female pair, and so are attracted to men and have irregular sex with them, and women who come from an original female-female pair, and so are attracted to women and have irregular sex with them. Aristophanes has a word for women who have irregular sex with men: *moicheutriai* = "adulteresses (with men)," which he has just used. (Shelley translated this word as "women . . . who intrigue with [men]," where "intrigue with" is a nineteenth-century euphemism for "commit adultery with.") But Aristophanes must coin a new, comic word, modeled on the normal word for "adulteress," for this new type of sexual irregularity he has categorized. So he invents *hetairistriai* = "adulteresses (with women)," based on *hetaira* = "female companion, concubine." The word appears nowhere else in classical Greek. (Since at 192b Aristophanes conceives of male-oriented men as still having spouses and children, this is also the way we should think of the female-oriented women. He thinks of them as wives who have little interest in their husbands, not as unmarried lesbians in the modern sense.)

192a such alone ever attain to political power: Aristophanes has his tongue firmly in his cheek here. Plato allows Aristophanes a gentle joke that only men who have been erotically involved in their youth with other men will amount to anything in political affairs, and is alluding to Aristophanes' much cruder version of the joke in *Clouds* 1084–1100: Unjust Speech routs Just Speech by pointing to the audience and observing that every prominent political man out there has been a pederast's plaything. Aristophanes is playing on the anxiety about the tension between masculine hardness and erotic softness evident in the other speakers. See 173d note.

192c sensual delights: The Greek word is *aphrodisia*, literally, "the things of Aphrodite," which is a regular Greek way of referring to genital sexual pleasure.

192d traces obscurely the footsteps of its obscure desire: The phrase translates a single Greek word, *ainit-testhai.* This verb, the root of our word "enigma," means to speak "enigmatically" or "indirectly" or "obscurely," and is especially appropriate to describing the riddling responses of oracles, as Aristophanes' reference to "divination" suggests. For other important references to "obscurity" with reference to Socrates, see 175e and 210a.

193b halved dice: Shelley's text reads *lispae*, which transliterates a Greek word meaning "halved dice." Greek erotic couples used such halved dice as love tokens, each keeping one half.

194a I confide in the fertility of their geniuses: The Greek reads simply, "I am confident." Shelley introduced terms from his own aesthetic vocabulary. See 187d note and 205c note.

195b Saturn and Japetus: Saturn was the father of Jupiter, who imprisoned him; Japetus was one of the elder Titans, father of Prometheus, also imprisoned by Jupiter. To call someone "more ancient than Saturn and Japetus" was a proverbial way of saying he was out-of-date.

197d Love divests us of all alienation from each other, and fills our vacant hearts with overflowing sympathy: This splendid line would more literally say, "Love empties us of alienation and fills us with kinship."

198c the head of the eloquent Gorgias: Socrates puns on the names of Gorgias, the great rhetorician whose style Agathon follows, and the Gorgon, a mythical monster which turned people to stone when they merely looked at it.

201d prophetess ... pestilence: Diotima is presented as a prophetess or diviner, and so as an adept of the art the

Greeks called *mantikê*. But here and at 211d, the Greek text Shelley translated had mistakenly substituted *mantikê* for *mantinikê* = "woman from Mantinea," Diotima's hometown. Plato clearly intends the pun. "The pestilence" refers to the devastating plague that struck Athens in 430 BC. We have no historical evidence for Diotima, and she is most likely a literary invention of Socrates (and Plato).

203b Metis: The name of Metis, the mother of Plenty, is a personification of practical cleverness; the word is often translated "cunning intelligence." It is the characteristic virtue of the wily Odysseus, for example. — Note that this account of Venus' birthday implies that Diotima is talking about the Pandemic Venus, and so in the terms defined by Pausanias (180d–e) about this younger, earthier Venus, a product of a mother as well as a father, not the older, heavenly, motherless Venus.

203d philosopher: Throughout this section, Diotima depends on the literal sense of "philosopher" as "lover of wisdom."

204e happy: The Greek word translated "happy" is *eudaimôn*; "happiness" is *eudaimonia*. Literally, to be happy is to have a good *daimôn*. Plato clearly wants us to have in mind the immediately preceding discussion of Eros as a great *daimôn*. Probably also relevant, though it is not mentioned in this dialogue, is Socrates' notorious "daimonic sign," a private oracle that came to him with advice from time to time.

205c the exercise of every inventive art is poetry, and all such artists poets: "artist" = *dêmiourgos* (see 187d note). In Greek, the general word for "making" is *poiêsis*, which in its more specialized sense, which is also its more common sense, means "poetry." Diotima is saying that every craft that brings something into existence is a type of making, so every craftsman is a type of maker, or poet. Shelley's word "inventive" might more precisely be "productive" or even "creative" here, since the emphasis is on making something exist. But he seems to have been influenced by 209a: "all poets, and all other artists [*dêmiourgoi*] who are creative and inventive [*heuretikoi*]." In this passage, "inventive" is a reasonable translation of *heuretikoi*, which comes from a verb meaning "to discover or contrive." Diotima is distinguishing crafts that require their practitioners to figure things out from crafts that require mere labor. But as a translation of the Greek, the aesthetic and imaginative connotations of "poetry," "invention," and "creation" are out of place in Diotima's speech, as they were in Eryximachus' earlier speech. Shelley apparently was playing on this ambiguity between the imaginative and the technical. See also 194a note. Shelley introduced his own aesthetic vocabulary into Diotima's speech in three more passages: 204a: "For this is the evil of ignorance, that he who has neither intelligence, nor virtue, *nor delicacy of sentiment*, imagines that he possesses all those things sufficiently" (emphasis added). Nothing in the Greek corresponds to the italicized phrase. 210a: "those perfect and sublime ends . . . trace the obscure depth of the subject." Nothing in the Greek corresponds to "sublime" or "obscure depth." 210d: "the wide ocean of intellectual beauty." "Hymn to Intellectual Beauty" is an important early poem of Shelley's, but "intellectual" does not appear in the Greek of this passage.

206d the Fate and the Juno Lucina: Two Roman goddesses associated with childbirth.

208d   Codrus: A legendary early king of Athens. When the city was attacked by Dorians, an oracle declared the invasion would be successful so long as Athens' king was not killed. Codrus disguised himself and attacked some Dorian soldiers to guarantee his own death and keep the city in the hands of his heirs.

209d   Lycurgus: The semi-legendary founder of the Lacedaemonian (that is, Spartan) constitution.

210a   beautiful forms . . . single form: Consistently throughout this section of Diotima's speech (210a–211c), Shelley avoided Diotima's straightforward talk about ascending from the love of beautiful "bodies" (*sômata*), softening the translation by substituting "forms." See also 211b, where Shelley wrote, "Ascending from a correct system of Love." Diotima actually says, "Ascending through practicing pederasty correctly." Shelley made the same substitution of "form" for "body" in the speeches of Pausanias (183e) and Agathon (196b). See note to 191c.

210e   on a sudden beholds a beauty: The suddenness of beauty's epiphany is reflected in this and three other passages, though Shelley's version doesn't bring this out: 213c: Socrates *suddenly* appears when Alcibiades least expects it. 217a: Alcibiades did *once* (*pot'*) see the divine images in Socrates. 223b: The revelers *suddenly* burst into Agathon's house.

211b   monoeidic: Here and at 211e, "monoeidic" transliterates rather than translates the Greek, which means "single-formed."

215a–b a certain statue . . . this statue . . . the images of the Gods: The word Shelley translates as "statue" is *eikôn,* which more accurately means "image" or "likeness." Alcibiades suggests he needs to use a likeness to get at the truth about Socrates. Contrast 200a, where Socrates responds to Agathon's appeal to what's likely (*eikos*, which Shelley renders as "I should imagine") by insisting on what follows "of necessity" rather than what is merely likely. "The images of the Gods" translates *agalmata theôn*, which more precisely means "statues (or figurines) of the gods."

215b   Silenuses . . . Marsyas: A "silenus" is another name for a satyr; in the singular, it can also be a proper name for the king of the satyrs. Marsyas was a satyr who challenged Apollo to a musical contest and was skinned alive for his presumption. His tunes were reputed to effect an ecstatic catharsis of morbid mental states.

215c   any musician, be he skilful or not: More accurately, "any flute-player, whether a good man or an inferior (*phaulê*) woman." For two other important references to female flute-players, see 176e and 212c.

215d   Pericles: The most important political leader in Athens for the three decades until his death from the plague in 429 BC, Pericles was also Alcibiades' legal guardian after his father died. He was reputed to be an extremely effective orator.

215e   Corybantic mysteries: Associated with the goddess Cybele, the Corybantic mysteries were a mythical cult characterized by ecstatic dance and cathartic music.

216a   Syrens: More commonly spelled "Sirens," these mythical creatures sang so beautifully that anyone who heard them died before he was able to tear himself away from them. Odysseus stopped up the ears of his crew so they could sail safely past the Sirens.

217a   even like the voice of a God: This phrase is an addition of Shelley's. Nothing in the Greek corresponds to it. Shelley may intend to compare Socrates' authority to that of an oracle or sudden epiphany. See notes to 192d and 210e.

218e   gold instead of brass: This phrase is proverbial for someone who makes a bad exchange. It comes from a scene in *Iliad* 6, where Glaucus and Diomedes meet on the battlefield only to discover they cannot fight since they have an old family connection. They decide to exchange gifts instead, but under the influence of Zeus, Glaucus foolishly exchanges his gold armor for Diomedes' bronze.

219e   less vulnerable by money than Ajax by iron: Ajax carried an enormous shield that made him virtually invulnerable to attack by sword or spear.

221a   Laches: An important Athenian general, Laches is the title character of a shorter Platonic dialogue focused on the education of the young and the nature of courage. Laches there tells this same story, and takes Socrates to be a moral expert based on his brave deeds.

221b   'he walked and darted his regards around with a majestic composure': Alcibiades quotes Aristophanes' description of Socrates' habitual gait and gaze from *Clouds* 362.

221c   Brasidas ... Nestor ... Antenor: Brasidas was an outstanding Spartan commander who died in 422 BC; the

Greek Nestor and the Trojan Antenor are presented in Homer as skilled public speakers.

222b Charmides, the son of Glauco, and Euthydemus, the son of Diodes: Charmides is the title character of a shorter Platonic dialogue focused on temperance and self-knowledge. He is portrayed as a young man whose physical beauty captivates Socrates. Charmides was the maternal uncle of Plato. The Glauco who is Charmides' father is Plato's maternal grandfather, after whom Glauco the brother of Plato, mentioned at 172c, was named. (Plato was named after his paternal grandfather Aristocles; "Plato" is a nickname, meaning "broad-shouldered.") Euthydemus is portrayed in Xenophon's *Memorabilia* as an attractive young man whose talents provoked Socrates' playful erotic interest. He is not the same man as the Euthydemus who was a professional sophist, after whom another Platonic dialogue is titled.

222d this Satyrical and Silenic drama: Socrates makes a rather complicated pun about Alcibiades' speech. At the dramatic competitions, playwrights presented four plays, three tragedies followed by a satyr play. The satyr play tended to present broad and deflating caricatures of the heroes of myth, which is how the English word "satire" was derived from "satyr." With its chorus of satyrs outfitted with huge phalluses, the satyr play provided a capstone to the dramatic festivals in keeping with the antic nature of Bacchus. (Even though the tone of a satyr play contrasted with the seriousness of the tragic trilogy it accompanied, the Greeks considered the ability to write such satyr plays independent of the ability to write comedies as such, as 223d shows.) So Socrates' pun has at least three levels. First, he refers simply to the fact that in characterizing him, Alcibiades made much use of comparisons to silenuses and satyrs. Second, he also figures Alcibiades as a competitor in a contest of speeches, and contrasts the comic tone of Alcibiades' speech with the seriousness of the others, especially his own. And third, he implicitly puts himself in the role of a mythical hero, caricatured in Alcibiades' speech as in a tragedian's satyr play.